D0002421

LIBERTY IN THE BALANCE:
CURRENT ISSUES IN CIVIL LIBERTIES

JC
599
.U5
W35
1981

Fifth Edition

H. FRANK WAY
Professor of Political Science
University of California, Riverside

McGRAW-HILL BOOK COMPANY

WITHDRAWN

New York   St. Louis   San Francisco   Auckland   Bogotá   Hamburg
Johannesburg   London   Madrid   Mexico   Montreal   New Delhi
Panama   Paris   São Paulo   Singapore   Sydney   Tokyo   Toronto

HIEBERT LIBRARY
Fresno Pacific College - M.B. Seminary
Fresno, CA 93702

63201

This book was set in Helvetica Light by Automated Composition Service, Inc.
The editors were Eric M. Munson and Barry Benjamin;
the production supervisor was Donna Piligra.
The cover was designed by Robin Hessel.
The Murray Printing Company was printer and binder.

Library of Congress Cataloging in Publication Data

Way, H   Frank.
    Liberty in the balance.

    (Foundations of American government and political
science)
    1. Civil rights—United States. I. Title.
II. Series.
JC599.U5W35   1981   323.4'0973   80-21039
ISBN 0-07-068661-0

**LIBERTY IN THE BALANCE: CURRENT ISSUES IN
CIVIL LIBERTIES**

Copyright © 1981, 1976, 1971, 1967, 1964 by McGraw-Hill, Inc. All rights reserved.
Printed in the United States of America. No part of this publication may be re-
produced, stored in a retrieval system, or transmitted, in any form or by any means,
electronic, mechanical, photocopying, recording, or otherwise, without the prior
written permission of the publisher.

    2 3 4 5 6 7 8 9 0   MUMU   8 9 8 7 6 5 4 3 2 1

FOUNDATIONS OF AMERICAN GOVERNMENT AND POLITICAL SCIENCE

Joseph P. Harris, Consulting Editor

Revisions and additions have been made to keep this series up to date and to enlarge its scope, but its purpose remains the same as it was on first publication: To provide a group of relatively short treatises dealing with major aspects of government in modern society. Each volume introduces the reader to a major field of political science through a discussion of important issues, problems, processes, and forces and includes at the same time an account of American political institutions. The author of each work is a distinguished scholar who specializes in and teaches the subjects covered. Together the volumes are well adapted to serving the needs of introductory courses in American government and political science.

Andrew Hacker: The Study of Politics: The Western Tradition and American Origins, 2D ED.

C. Herman Pritchett: The American Constitutional System, 5TH ED.

Hugh A. Bone and Austin Ranney: Politics and Voters, 5TH ED.

Rowland Egger: The President of the United States, 2ND ED.

Joseph P. Harris: Congress and the Legislative Process, 2D ED.

> (The two books listed above were revised and enlarged from materials contained in the first edition of *The President and Congress* by Rowland Egger and Joseph P. Harris.)

Charles R. Adrian: Governing Our Fifty States and Their Communities, 4TH ED.

H. Frank Way: Liberty in the Balance: Current Issues in Civil Liberties, 5TH ED.

МWAЯ DНТIW

LIBERTY
IN THE
BALANCE:

CURRENT ISSUES
IN CIVIL LIBERTIES

D0219535

CONTENTS

PREFACE

It is the common fate of the indolent to see their rights become a prey to the active. The condition upon which God hath given liberty to man is eternal vigilance; which condition if he break, servitude is at once the consequence of his crime and the punishment of his guilt.

John P. Curran, 1790

The words of John Curran are as timely for this generation as they were for the 1790s. Yet a recognition of the importance of eternal vigilance does not solve the conundrum posed to each generation: where and how must we be vigilant?

Each day in some city council room, or in a legislative body, or in a police station the liberty of free people will weigh in the balance. Each day decisions are made, policies adopted, actions taken that can narrow the scope of human freedom. All too frequently, when liberty is in the balance the attention of free people is focused elsewhere. The climate of public indifference to the "petty" invasions of liberty, to the "minor" violations of justice, carries with it the winds of tyranny—petty and colossal. Freedom is never secure where a people are indifferent to arbitrary police power or when they silently agree that conventional standards of private morality are more important than freedom of the press.

But even when local opinion is raised against the invasions of liberty, the frequent conclusion is that such issues should be solved by lawyers and judges. Yet liberty is not exclusively a legal matter. Liberty is an integral part of the politics of citizenship, and the forum for its preservation is not just in a court of law; the first forum is the library board meeting, the city council meeting, the party precinct meeting, the picket line, or the sit-in. As the late Justice Robert H. Jackson once observed, "the attitude of a society and of its organized political forces rather than its legal machinery is the controlling force in the character of free institutions."

It would be wrong to infer, however, that legal-constitutional rules do not play an important part in the allocation of liberty. Liberty is in part a socioeconomic artifact, and due consideration should be given to the environmental context of freedom. The variables are probably enormous—

income distribution, educational attainment, population density, ethnic complexion of population, quality of legal institutions, occupational distribution, national security, quality of the media, and so forth. But liberty is also an artifact of the law, perhaps not as much as was assumed fifty years ago, but rather more so than the behavioralist generation was prepared to acknowledge. The rules of constitutional law do make a difference, although not necessarily on a uniform basis. The rules do set certain broad boundaries for the resolution of policy differences. Justice Holmes to the contrary notwithstanding, general propositions are indeed important in the resolution of concrete cases. While one need not accept a mechanical view of the law, still the attention given to constitutional doctrine in courts, legislative chambers, and other arenas suggests that the rule of law is more than a fiction created by Blackstone.

If constitutional rules can make a difference in the quantity and quality of freedom, then we should continue to insist that the government respond to the constitutional issues that arise in a changing society. All agencies of the government share in this broad responsibility, but no agency has a greater role here than the judiciary. It is sometimes a role that the judiciary would prefer to ignore, albeit in the name of judicial self-restraint. Self-restraint, however, can never justify judicial abdication of the responsibilities that flow from the Bill of Rights. We need not fear "government-by-judiciary" nearly as much as we need fear a government with only parchment liberties.

Over the years my colleagues have listened, with more patience than perhaps I deserved, as I ruminated about constitutional developments, and I thank them, especially Professors Edwin Gaustad and Don Brown. Finally I dedicate this volume to Charlotte Beaty for a debt I cannot repay.

H. FRANK WAY

LIBERTY IN THE BALANCE:

CURRENT ISSUES IN CIVIL LIBERTIES

1 DISCRIMINATION IN AMERICA

RACIAL JUSTICE

It is now over a quarter of a century since the Supreme Court handed down its decision in *Brown v. Topeka Board of Education*.[1] In striking down governmentally imposed racial segregation in public education, the Supreme Court riveted the nation's attention on the constitutional rights of black Americans. The Court held that for the government to separate pupils in schools on the basis of race amounted to denial of the equal protection of the laws promised to all persons by the constitution.[2]

The *Brown* decision was the sharpest single blow ever delivered to the *legal* facade of racial prejudice in America, and as such, it is one of the great watersheds of constitutional history. It inspired a mass movement, and its ramifications in the political, social, and economic life of the nation have been profound. Yet *Brown* did not promise an end to inequality nor did it promise an end to racial segregation. Although *Brown* was to come to mean many things, its focus was narrow. All that *Brown* attempted to do was to strike down the *legal foundation* of racial segregation, initially in public education and subsequently in public facilities.

Of course *Brown* was to inspire goals well beyond its constitutional rule, goals that were captured in the civil rights movement of the late 1950s and early 1960s. The movement produced a series of heroes, most notably Martin Luther King Jr., as it moved from legal attacks in courtrooms to demonstrations. In just over a decade, from the Montgomery bus boycott in 1955 to the death of King in 1968, the civil rights movement changed the course of American history. During that brief period the final assault on Jim Crowism was successfully launched and new horizons opened for racial and ethnic minorities in the political, social, and economic arenas of American life. It is, of course, an unfinished revolution, yet its accomplishments are notable.

---

[1] *Brown v. Topeka Board of Education*, 347 U.S. 483 (1954).
[2] The Fourteenth Amendment's equal protection clause applies to the states, and the federal equivalent of this clause in the school desegregation case was the due process clause of the Fifth Amendment; see *Bolling v. Sharpe*, 347 U.S. 497 (1954)

SOCIAL AND ECONOMIC JUSTICE

The civil rights movement has helped to make it possible for increasing numbers of black Americans to achieve a higher degree of economic security. The employment opportunity provision of the 1964 Civil Rights Act, coupled with other actions by the federal government, has enabled thousands of blacks to improve their standard of living. However, as compared with whites, black Americans have yet to achieve parity. On practically any scale that one might use to measure social and economic justice, blacks are still far behind whites—in educational attainment, income, quality of housing, occupational status, and employment. Yet in each category the gap is being narrowed.[3]

INCOME

While the picture of black income is no longer as bleak as it once was, there still remains a wide gap between black and white income. Furthermore, the rise in black income is somewhat misleading because the rise has not been uniformly distributed. For example, from 1947 to 1974 the ratio of aggregate black family income to aggregate white family income rose from 56 percent to 71 percent, or from $3,500 to $7,810. Although the ratio just noted is promising, aggregate income data do not reveal anything about income distribution. The latter can be seen by reference to the median income data, and here the figure is anything but promising.[4] In 1974, the ratio of median black family income to median white family income was only 58 percent. (By 1977 the ratio had fallen to 57 percent.) The contrast between the aggregate and median data reveals a pronounced unevenness in the distribution of rising black income. For example, by 1974 young black husband-and-wife wage-earners (husbands under thirty-five years of age) had achieved virtual income parity with their white counterparts, and, indeed, in the North and West their joint incomes exceeded the income of comparable white couples by 7 percent. Yet the relative prosperity enjoyed by younger black husband-and-wife families is in sharp contrast to the continued poverty of a large percentage of the black population. Thus, in 1974 slightly over 31 percent of the black population was below the poverty level, in sharp contrast to just under 9 percent of the white population. Furthermore, within the black community the poverty rate was more pronounced within two groups—the young, that is, children under eighteen years of age, and the old, that is, persons sixty-five years and over. Young blacks had a poverty rate of 41 percent in 1974, and for older blacks the rate was 36 percent. Among young female-headed families the picture was even grimmer—a 1974 poverty rate of approximately 63 percent. In short, the trend over

[3]Unless otherwise noted, all data reported below are from U.S. Bureau of the Census, *The Social and Economic Status of the Black Population in the United States, 1790-1978*, 1979.
[4]Aggregate family income data are arrived at by dividing the total income by the total number of families, whereas median family income data are determined by finding the exact midpoint in an income series.

the past two decades has been toward a rising black middle-class couple with substantial poverty among the young and the old.[5]

EMPLOYMENT AND UNEMPLOYMENT

From 1954 until 1965 black employment increased at a rate faster than white employment. In recent years, however, the rate of increase of black employment has fallen behind that of white employment. The 1970–1975 rate of increase for black employment was 4.8 percent in contrast to a 7.7 percent increase for whites. In part, this may be a reflection of the pressure on employment caused by a more rapid increase in the black labor force, which in turn is a reflection of a higher black fertility rate. While the black fertility rate continues to be greater than the white fertility rate, nonetheless, it declined by approximately 50 percent from 1950 to 1975.

Declining fertility rates among black women may eventually reduce the pressure on the job market. In the meantime, however, blacks continue to experience substantially higher rates of unemployment than whites. Indeed, from 1948 to 1975 blacks generally had an unemployment rate double that of whites. By 1977 white unemployment was 6.2 percent in contrast to 13.9 percent for blacks. More alarming, however, is the continued high rate of unemployment among black teenagers, which stood at approximately 40 percent in 1977, an increase of twenty percentage points in twenty years.

HOUSING

Throughout the 1950s and 1960s, as whites abandoned the central cities and moved into new suburban housing, often with government aid, it became apparent that housing was a major problem for minorities. Although racial integration in housing was never a major thrust of the civil rights movement, equal access to housing without regard to race was on the civil rights agenda. Initially the goal was to remove legal barriers to open housing and subsequently to stop the government from actively supporting racial homogeneity in residential housing. In 1948 in *Shelley v. Kraemer* racially restrictive covenants were held to be non-enforceable in the courts,[6] and almost concurrently the Federal Housing Administration discontinued its previous policy of actively encouraging residential segregation. A similar policy of neutrality was adopted by the Veterans Administration. But government toleration of open housing did little to alter the situation. Between 1946 and 1959 less than 2 percent of the FHA subdivision housing went to minorities.[7] In 1962 President Kennedy issued an executive order prohibiting discrimination

[5]A completely accurate picture would also point out that poverty among younger and older blacks has steadily declined since 1959; the rise of a black middle class has been challenged in Robert Hill, "The Illusion of Black Progress," *Social Policy*, vol. 9, no. 14, 1978.

[6]*Shelley v Kraemer*, 334 U.S. 1 (1948).

[7]Simpson Lawson, "Above Property Rights," U.S. Commission On Civil Rights, December 1972.

in federally assisted housing. Two years later, the Civil Rights Act of 1964 incorporated the order into Title VI. Finally, Congress passed a comprehensive open-housing policy in the Civil Rights Act of 1968. Under the 1968 legislation racial discrimination is prohibited in the sale or rental of all federally owned or operated dwellings and in most dwellings secured by federal loan-insurance programs. The only major exemptions apply to single-family homes sold or rented by the owner without the assistance of an agent and to certain small owner-occupied rooming houses or apartments. Also in 1968 the Supreme Court breathed new life into an 1866 Reconstruction act that stipulates that all citizens have the same right to inherit, purchase, lease, sell, hold, and convey property. The Court construed the act to bar all racial discrimination, public and private, in the sale or rental of property.[8]

In addition to the 1968 legislation, Congress passed the Equal Credit Opportunity Act of 1974. The 1974 legislation makes it unlawful for creditors to discriminate against an applicant for credit on the basis of race, color, religion, national origin, sex, marital status, or age. (The age limitation assumes the applicant is otherwise legally qualified to enter into a contract.)

The legislation of 1968 and 1974 now makes it possible for racial and ethnic minorities to have equal *legal* access to housing. Whether legal equality can be translated into improved housing remains to be seen. However, there are some indicators that suggest that the quality of housing for racial minorities has improved. Perhaps the most important single indicator is the increase in owner, as distinct from renter, occupancy of housing by blacks, which increased from 19 percent in 1940 to 36 percent in 1970. However, on a comparative basis, blacks are still far less likely to own their homes than are whites. The white owner-occupancy rate in 1970 was 64 percent. Two other indicators of housing quality should be mentioned; one concerns the improvement in overcrowding in black housing. In 1940, 52 percent of black urban renters occupied housing with more than one person per room. By 1970 the rate had declined to 27 percent. The comparable white rate in 1970 was 10 percent. The second quality indicator that can be noted is the decline of black-occupied housing units lacking some or all plumbing facilities. In 1940, three out of four black housing units lacked some or all plumbing facilities. By 1970 the rate had declined to 16 percent, a rate that was, nonetheless, four times as high as the rate for whites.

Based on the above indicators, it is possible to conclude that at least the quality of black housing in the United States is improving. However, racial discrimination in housing opportunities continues to be a problem. In 1974 the United States Commission on Civil Rights concluded that federal agencies were having little impact in resolving serious problems in discrimination in housing.[9] And again in 1979, the same

---

[8]*Jones v. Alfred Mayer Co.*, 392 U.S. 409 (1968).

[9]U.S. Commission on Civil Rights, *The Federal Civil Rights Enforcement Effort—1974*, Washington, D.C., vol. 2, p. 328; for an in-depth study of racial discrimination in housing, see Joe T. Darden, *Afro-Americans in Pittsburgh: The Residential Segregation of a People*. Michigan State University, East Lansing, 1979.

agency noted that current legislation failed to provide for adequate enforcement mechanisms to ensure fair housing, and even within this inadequate framework the federal agencies were not carrying out their duty to insure equal housing opportunities.[10]

OCCUPATIONAL STATUS

Until 1960 the relative occupation status of black and white workers had remained the same for fifty years. Beginning in 1960, however, the rate of increase in occupational status for black workers was three times as rapid as the rate of status increase for white workers. From 1963 to 1977, the percentage of black males in white-collar positions increased from 15 to 23 percent and for black females from 21 to 44 percent. Blacks have also experienced similar increases in the better-paying blue-collar positions, rising, for example, from 10.7 percent of the black male workers in craft positions in 1963 to 16 percent in 1977. (See Table 1.)

Occupational upgrading of blacks was most notable among the younger and better educated, particularly those with some college education. It was most pronounced among better-educated black females. In the years from 1963 to 1977, the percentage of black females employed as domestics declined from 34 percent to 10 percent, whereas in the same years the percentage of black females in clerical positions rose from 10 percent to 25 percent, and black females in professional and technical positions increased from 8 percent to 13 percent.

On the other hand the relative position of blacks to whites in some of the most prestigious professional positions has remained stable. For example, the number of blacks as a percentage of the total number of teachers in America has remained at 8 percent for approximately twenty years. Similarly while there was a 30 percent increase from 1960 to

[10]U.S. Commission on Civil Rights. *The Federal Fair Housing Enforcement Effort*, 1979.

TABLE 1 Occupations of employed men and women, 1977 (Numbers in thousands, annual averages)

	Men		Women	
Occupation	*Black*	*White*	*Black*	*White*
Total employed	4,496	48,578	3,887	32,156
Percent	100	100	100	100
White-collar workers	23	42	44	66
Blue-collar workers	58	45	18	14
Service workers	17	8	37	19
Farm workers	3	4	1	1

Source: *The Social and Economic Status of the Black Population in the United States*, U.S. Bureau of the Census, 1978, Table 164.

1970 in the number of black doctors, only 2 percent of all doctors are blacks, and this percentage has remained the same since 1910.

EDUCATION

For all of the delays and disappointments in the desegregation of public schools there are, nonetheless, numerous indicators of dramatic improvement in the formal education attainment of blacks, as seen in Table 2. Black illiteracy has declined from 61 percent in 1890 to 4 percent in 1969, and the median years of schooling completed by blacks has increased from 5.7 years in 1940 to 10.9 years in 1975. Even more dramatic is the substantial increase in black college-age enrollment, increasing from 10 percent in 1965 to just over 20 percent in 1970. However, as indicated in Table 2, there is still a wide disparity in the ratio of black to white income based on the number of years of school completed.

CLOSING THE GAPS

While there remain wide disparities between blacks and whites the facts are, nonetheless, more complex than is revealed by a quick glance at income, employment, housing, and education data. To some the data may suggest that the civil rights movement was a failure; that it not only did not end social and economic injustice, but it did not even provide a secure foundation for ending racial injustice. Doubtless, the movement did not bring an end to racial injustice in the social and economic arenas, but it is equally true that the movement had a kind of catalytic impact on government and the private sector. For example, the

TABLE 2 Ratio of median income of family heads 25 years old and over, by years of school completed, 1974 (revised), 1975, and 1976 (in 1976 dollars)

Years of school completed by family head and race	1974*	1975	1976
Ratio: Black to White Total family heads, 25 years old and over	0.61	0.63	0.62
Elementary:			
Less than 8 years	0.79	0.85	0.78
8 years	0.74	0.74	0.73
High school:			
1 to 3 years	0.61	0.65	0.62
4 years	0.73	0.69	0.69
College:			
1 to 3 years	0.83	0.81	0.84
4 years or more	0.84	0.90	0.89

*Revised.

Source: *The Social and Economic Status of the Black Population in the United States*, U.S. Bureau of the Census, 1978, p. 197.

emergence of a young black middle class is not an unimportant gain. Whether such a gain will provide a secure foundation for further advances depends in no small way on the resolution of the continuing impasse in black education.

SCHOOL DESEGREGATION: THE CONTINUING IMPASSE

Given the long-standing nature of America's racial problems, it is not particularly surprising that the 1954 *Brown* decision still arouses controversy.[11] Indeed, as Table 3 indicates, the level of public school racial segregation remains high, especially in areas outside of the South and border states. Of course, controversy has not been a stranger to racial issues in the United States, nor to the *Brown* policy. From the outset the *Brown* decision was plagued by problems that defied its moral clarity. Shortly after the 1954 decision, the South embarked on a decade-long program of legislative and executive resistance to the mandate of desegregation. Yet ironically, if the death knell of school desegregation is being sounded today, the toll is primarily heard outside the South. The toll of school desegregation is being sounded in Los Angeles and Boston and Dayton and in Chicago, and the name of the mournful tune is "busing."

The Reverend Jesse Jackson may well have been correct when he said: "It ain't the bus, it's us." But widespread anti-busing sentiment cannot be dismissed as simply crypto-racism. Anti-busing sentiment may well feed on continued racial and ethnic prejudice, but to dismiss the sentiment as mere bigotry is to ignore an otherwise complex issue. Both the practical and moral justifications for school integration have been undermined over the past fifteen years. The old mythology of "black and white together" has been challenged by the presumed failure of the *Brown* decision and its progeny to eliminate racial inequality and racial prejudice. Indeed, over the past fifteen years a considerable body of research, some not particularly sound, has emerged to question whether integration has had any significant and beneficial impact on black academic achievement.[12] Furthermore, the changing racial composition of American cities often creates major logistical and legal problems in framing desegregation plans. Finally, large-scale busing of white students creates a dilemma for many white parents who were otherwise positive or at least passive about school desegregation.[13] Previously, where busing involved dispersing racial and ethnic minority students throughout a majority white school system, few objections were raised. When, as is the case often today, the reverse occurs, that is, the plans call for substantial busing of a white student

[11]*Brown v. Topeka Board of Education*, 347 U.S. 483 (1954).
[12]See, for example, Norman Miller and Harold Gerard, "How Busing Failed in Riverside," *Psychology Today*, June 1976, p. 67; David Armor, "The Evidence on Busing," *Public Interest*, no. 29, p. 99, 1972; compare, however, Thomas Pettigrew et al., "Pierced Armor," *Integrated Education*, vol. 10, no. 6, p. 5, 1972.
[13]See Jon Alston and Ben Crouch, "White Acceptance of Three Degrees of School Desegregation," *Phylon*, vol. 39, no. 3, p. 216, 1978.

TABLE 3 1976 projected average level of segregation for various minorities and regions*

Racial/Ethnic Group	Northeast	North Central	Border	Southeast	West South Central	West	Nation
Blacks	.39	.47	.23	.17	.28	.34	.30
Hispanics	.34	.04	.04	.20	.14	.15	.17
Asians/Pacific Islanders	.01	.01	.04	.02	.02	.05	.03
American Indians/ Alaskan Natives	.01	.28	.00	.22	.02	.08	.11
All Minorities	.34	.37	.21	.16	.20	.18	.24
Number of districts surveyed	539	784	108	882	737	566	3616

*In this analysis, level of segregation is described as low level if the index is 0.0–0.19, moderate level if the index is 0.20–0.49, and high level if the index is 0.50 or greater.

Source: *Desegregation of the Nation's Public Schools: A Status Report*, U.S Commission on Civil Rights, February 1979.

population among a school population now heavily populated by blacks and browns, many white parents object. Part of the objection is based simply on busing white children away from their neighborhood schools, even though blacks have long faced a similar requirement. Yet another aspect of the problem, and one far more difficult to resolve, is the fear among many white parents that their children's academic achievement will suffer, especially where it is likely that the white students will be placed in classes with substantial numbers of academic low achievers. Indeed, desegregation studies have found a correlation between white nonattendance, the so-called white flight, at assigned black majority schools and the distance of the bus ride, plus the reading and math achievement scores of the assigned schools.[14] In short, it is now widely acknowledged that "white flight" has occured in conjunction with many school desegregation plans,[15] and at least part of the explanation for this involves white fears about academic achievement in schools with large minority populations. Yet, there is simply no direct evidence, especially in the form of longitudinal studies, that would confirm or deny these fears.[16]

Beyond the issues of "white flight" and black and white academic achievement, there is an additional problem, and that is the growing isolation of the judiciary in matters of desegregation. When the *Brown* decision was decided in 1954, the Supreme Court stood alone, and it was almost ten years before the executive and legislative branches became effective partners in launching major programs to eliminate racial inequality. Indeed, it was the passage of Title VI of the Civil Rights Act of 1964, conferring power on the executive branch to withhold federal funds from schools practicing racial discrimination, that finally gave the federal government an effective power base to ensure compliance with desegregation orders. By 1974, however, congressional support for desegregation had been substantially eroded. For example, 1974 Congress passed the Esch Amendment forbidding federal courts or executive agencies from ordering pupil transportation to any school other than the closest or next closest to the pupil's residence. The Esch Amendment is only one example of a series of congressional attacks on school busing in integration cases. The growing disenchantment with busing, in Congress, coupled with a reluctance to push school desegregation in certain quarters of the executive branch, has had the effect of once again placing on the shoulders of the judiciary the burden of providing leadership on a politically sensitive and constitutionally complex issue. The courts have not always been equal to the task.

While the *Brown* decision had a strong moral appeal and offered hope of improving black educational achievement through integration, the decision did not rest on such hope or moral appeal. Rather, the de-

[14]See testimony of David Armor in the Los Angeles School Desegregation Case, *Los Angeles Times*, November 6, 1979, sect. B, p. 1; on the issue of "white flight," see Diane Ravitch, "The White Flight Controversy," *Public Interest*, no. 51, p. 135, Spring 1978.

[15]See Christine Rossell, "White flight: Pros and Cons," *Social Policy*, vol. 9, no. 3, p. 46, 1978.

[16]Although one would be entitled to speculate that since academic achievement evidently bears far less relationship to the school setting than it does to home background, the fears of white parents would not be justified. See James S. Coleman et al., *Equality of Educational Opportunity*, U.S. Office of Education, 1966.

cision rested firmly on a reasonably narrow constitutional rule, namely, that the equal protection clause of the Fourteenth Amendment forbids a government agency from separating public school pupils on the basis of race. As in all equal protection litigation, the predicate upon which relief had to be based was *government* or *state* action in denying a plaintiff the equal protection of the laws. The predicate was necessary since the equal protection clause states that "No state shall . . . deny to any person equal protection of the laws." Thus, the restriction is on state action rather than on the action of private individuals. At the time of the *Brown* decision the government's involvement in and indeed sponsorship of, a dual school system for blacks and whites in Southern and border states was clear and unequivocal. The government's role in sponsoring segregation in these states could not be contested for the simple reason that it was written in state statutes and state constitutions that constituted the legal framework for segregated schools. Of course, these statutes and constitutional provisions now have either been repealed or declared unconstitutional. The old legal facade is gone, but racial and ethnic separatism in public schools is a fact of life in virtually all areas of the nation that have any substantial minority population. Thus, today the question of whether racial imbalances are the result of government action, that is, whether racial imbalances are de jure, poses a more difficult evidentiary problem for the courts than was once the case. Whatever the merits may be of a social policy of maintaining racially balanced schools, we must not forget that the *Brown* decision was aimed, and constitutionally could only be aimed, at providing equitable remedies for de jure, or government imposed, racial segregation in public schools.

Few would contest today that a considerable amount of racial imbalance in urban schools is the byproduct of private choices made in housing. These private choices were unquestionably constrained by certain government decisions regarding the location and the availability of such things as public housing, freeways and other forms of public transportation, and mortgage credit. Yet housing choices are still essentially private choices and as such are not covered by the Fourteenth Amendment's prohibition on a *state* denying equal protection of its law to all persons. Thus, today desegregation suits often pose difficult problems in evidence. For example, can it be demonstrated by the evidence submitted in a particular school district case that the racial imbalance in the local schools is the product of action by the government, or rather is it largely, or even exclusively, the de facto result of racial patterns in housing? The factual inquiry that must be conducted by the trial courts to resolve these questions has become increasingly rarefied as the Supreme Court has moved further away from the *Brown* predicate, that is, government sponsorship of a dual school system.

THE SUPREME COURT AND
SCHOOL DESEGREGATION

While it would be unfair to place the current impasse in school busing and desegregation solely at the feet of the justices of the Supreme Court, they do bear some responsibility for the situation. The problem in part can be traced back to the Court's 1968 decision in *Green v. The County School Board*.[17] This decision arose out of a Virginia school desegregation case and as such involved an entire school system that at one time was operated de jure on a racially segregated basis. The school board had continued its dual school system long after the *Brown* decision and had made no effort to dismantle segregated schools until, in 1965, it faced the threat of losing federal funds. The board then offered a so-called freedom of choice plan that would have allowed most pupils to make a positive choice as to the school they wished to attend. Since the plan placed the responsibility for making a choice on the pupils rather than the school board, the result was predictable. No white pupil chose to attend the all-black combined elementary-high school, and only 115 out of the 740 black pupils chose to attend the previously all-white combined elementary-high school. The Court unanimously held that this "freedom of choice" plan was insufficient to discharge the board's responsibility under the *Brown* decision. Up to this point, there is nothing particularly startling about the Court's conclusion. The case was a rather typical charade by a Southern school system to ignore the mandate of *Brown*. What is exceptional about *Green* is a single sentence in which the Court said that de jure segregated schools were under "the affirmative duty to take whatever steps might be necessary to convert to a unitary system in which racial discrimination would be eliminated, root and branch."[18] In short, the Court appeared to indicate that the equal protection clause not only forbids positive state acts of racial segregation, but that it also affirmatively requires racial segregation, that is, conversion to a nonracial school system.

Within the context of a previously state mandated dual school system, the *Green* decision made sense. It would have been difficult to argue that Southern and border states were required under *Brown* only to drop the legal facade of school segregation. Without any administrative effort to dismantle what they had created, the Southern and border state school systems would have remained largely segregated. Simply dropping the legal requirement of racially separate schools would not have, without more, changed anything. Thus, the shift in *Green* from *desegregation* to affirmative *integration* may seem only a semantic problem, but it involves more than a subtle shift in language. For example, it does not necessarily follow that a governmentally nonsegregated system will be a nonracial system, at least to the extent that there will be no racial patterns in the distribution of the pupil population. Perhaps the Court could not have anticipated the problems suggested by its language in *Green*. In any event, three years later the Court compounded the problem.

In 1971, in *Swann v. Charlotte-Mecklenburg Board of Education* the Court had before it a series of contested plans for desegrating a large countywide school system that included the City of Charlotte as well as Mecklenburg County, North Carolina.[19] The system included 60,000 white pupils and 24,000 black pupils. However, 87 percent of the black pupils lived in Charlotte. This immediately raised the question of whether

[17]*Green v. The County School Board*, 391 U.S. 430.
[18]Ibid., pp. 437–438.
[19]*Swan v. Charlotte-Mecklenburg Board of Education*, 402 U.S. 1 (1971).

segregation in this school district could be totally attributed to the previous legal ban on integrated schools, or whether a substantial degree of de facto segregation would have been present even in the absence of the legal framework that had supported desegregated schools. This is a potentially explosive issue, and the *Swann* decision did not address it. Instead, the Court upheld a plan that involved large-scale two-way busing of inner-city and suburban pupils, including the pairing of nine inner-city elementary schools with twenty-four suburban elementary schools. Additionally, the Court specifically sanctioned target racial quotas. Although the Court warned against attempting to use desegregation cases to accomplish broader social goals in race relations,[20] nonetheless, the Court appeared to sanction the greatest possible degree of integration without specific regard to any causal relationship between the current racial imbalances and the prior de jure framework for segregated schools.[21]

The *Swann* and *Green* requirement of an affirmative duty to produce an integrated school system arose out of Southern school systems that had at one time mandated dual schools. As indicated above, in both cases the Court ignored the issue of the degree of racial imbalance that would have obtained even in the absence of the dual school system. Nor was the issue raised in any concurring or dissenting opinion. Indeed, it was not until 1973, in a Denver, Colorado, case, *Keyes v. The School District*, that the issue first surfaced.[22] In the *Keyes* decision the trial court had found intentional acts of segregation only in a portion of the Denver school district. The trial court rejected the mere fact of racial imbalance in other areas as establishing proof of intentional segregation. The Supreme Court modified the trial court's position and ruled instead that where the plaintiffs prove de jure segregation in a substantial portion of a district, "it is only common sense to conclude that there exists a predicate for a finding of the existence of a dual school system."[23] Thus, a factual determination of intentional segregation in a meaningful part of a school district creates "a *prima facie* case of unlawful segregative design on the part of the school authorities and shifts to those authorities the burden of proving that other segregated schools within the system are not also the result of intentionally segregative action."[24] The Court went on, in *Swann*, to place a difficult, perhaps even impossible, evidentiary burden on such school districts. The Court said that in rebutting a prima facie case a school district may not rely merely on logical, racially neutral explanations of its prior actions but must *prove* that segregative intent was not a factor. In short, a prima facie case of segregative intent in one area of a district taints the remaining areas, and consequently the school district is then forced to prove a negative, a requirement that is likely to give full employment to lawyers and expert witnesses. As Justice Rehnquist noted in dissent, proving the intent of a public body

[20]Ibid., p. 23.

[21]Ibid., p. 26; and see companion case, *David v. Board of School Commissioners*, 402 U.S. 33, 38 (1971).

[22]*Keyes v. The School District*, 413 U.S. 189.

[23]Ibid., p. 201.

[24]Ibid., p. 208.

when it performs an act is difficult at best, and in the case of elective school boards with ever-changing membership, it is even more difficult.[25]

The *Keyes* decision, as a continuation of the *Green, Swann* "affirmative duty" to integrate requirement, has weakened the distinction between de jure and de facto segregation. The weakening is more than a semantic loss since it contributes to a diminution of the constitutional basis of the *Brown* decision. Furthermore, the absence in the *Keyes* decision of any precise guidelines for trial courts in determining "segregative intent" is likely to support endless litigation in which contending parties will never be satisfied of the accuracy of the trial judge's factual determination.

The Supreme Court has not directly addressed what is the fundamental issue in many Northern school desegregation cases. Namely, is it an act of "segregative intent" for a school board to continue to maintain what has heretofore been a racially neutral neighborhood school policy in the face of shifting racial patterns in housing? In other words, are schools boards under some affirmative constitutional duty to respond with an integration plan in order to prevent a neighborhood school from becoming a segregated school as a result of racial shifts in housing? Stated otherwise, does de facto segregation become de jure segregation if a school board should have realized that the *foreseeable consequences of taking no action would be an increase in segregated schools*? If the answer to these questions is yes, then there is no longer a viable distinction between governmentally imposed, or de jure segregation and the segregation that may occur as a natural consequence of racially distinct neighborhoods coupled with the policy of neighborhood schools. This is not to suggest, however, that Northern school districts have always pursued racially neutral policies and that racial housing patterns are the only explanatory variable in Northern school segregation. Given the historic extent of racial prejudice in the United States, it seems quite probable that when the black population of Northern school districts rose substantially, some school boards did engage in manipulative practices that were racially motivated. It is not open to debate that such practices are unconstitutional; what is an open question is whether a "cognitive omission" by school boards, that is, consciously doing nothing, amounts to a denial of equal protection of the laws. There is some indication that the Court thinks it does.

In a 1979 case, *Columbus Board of Education v. Penick*, the Court adopted a trial court's finding that the Columbus, Ohio, school board was operating, prior to the *Brown* decision in 1954, a dual school system.[26] The trial court's finding was based on "cognitive acts or omissions" in the period from 1909 to 1943, and thus, after 1954 the board was under an affirmative duty to integrate. When new school sites were selected in Columbus after 1954, they presented the board with what the trial court termed "integrative opportunities," which if not seized became "cognitive omissions." The *Columbus* decision not only abandoned the critical element of discriminatory purpose in assessing official acts, it also sanctioned a refusal by a trial court to make any determination of the linkage between remote acts and present conditions of racial imbalance. What needs to be determined in a desegregation case is whether current conditions of racial imbalance have a causal linkage to prior manipulative practices that were racially motivated. Furthermore, the factual inquiry should be discrete as to the degree to which a current condition can be attributed solely or partially to prior constitutional violation. A high degree of particularity is necessary in order to ensure that the remedy or order does not exceed the violation. System-wide orders for school desegregation which do not rest on the system-wide impact of prior violations exceed the equitable powers of federal district courts. In summary, the Supreme Court, as it approaches racial imbalances in public schools, must develop a precise methodology for determining constitutional violations under the *Brown* decision. The predicate for a *Brown*-type integration order must be official acts of racial discrimination and not simply a de facto condition of racially identifiable schools. Racial balance in public schools may be a desirable social policy. It is not, however, a constitutional requirement.

A return to the de jure requirements of school integration orders is not without risks. It could be misconstrued as a retreat from *Brown* rather than a return to *Brown*. Given the special historical role played by the Supreme Court in matters of racial desegregation, a return to the *Brown* predicate of de jure segregation could have negative significance, particularly if there were reasons to question the Court's motivation. Yet a continuation of the present fruitless struggle to achieve racial balance is also not without its own risks.

CONCLUSION

Racial and ethnic discrimination is an insidious disease that has plagued the United States far too long. As a society the United States must continue the often painfully slow process of ending such discrimination, and the government has an important role to play in the process. The government cannot abandon the moral requirements of the *Brown* decision in any area—housing, employment, or education. Yet it does not serve the moral foundation of *Brown* or constitutional policy to engage in what the public perceives to be factually tortured integration orders that cause massive dislocations of pupils. The strength of *Brown* rested not on its condemnation of racial prejudice per se, but rather its condemnation of governmentally inspired racial prejudice. That remains a substantial and important goal, and the judiciary should ensure that in accomplishing this goal it does not undermine public acceptance of the goal by attempting to go beyond the promise of the equal protection clause.

For many people racial balance in public education remains an important objective. If our society is to move beyond color, then achieving a degree of racial balance in the schools can be an important step in that direction. The objective, however, is not well served by tortured constructions of the equal protection clause. No public school board should be allowed to engage in racially motivated manipulative practices, and the federal courts should offer remedies appropriate to any such violation, but the remedies should not go beyond the violation. That is, the remedies should not attempt to eradicate de facto segregation under the thin disguise of "cognitive omissions" and "integrative opportunities missed."

AFFIRMATIVE ACTION IN PUBLIC HIGHER EDUCATION AND PRIVATE EMPLOYMENT

Responsible public officials have long recognized that some remedial actions are necessary in order to accelerate the rate of advancement for minorities. One such method is the so-called affirmative action program, which attempts to compensate for prior discrimination by active programs of recruitment into such areas as skilled trades and professional occupations. Often these programs have been legally challenged as nothing more than "reverse discrimination," that is, programs that benefit minorities at the expense of a majority, such as whites or males.

Racial and ethnic discrimination in the private sector is not controlled by the equal protection clause since this clause applies only to state action. It is, however, the subject of federal legislation. The basic federal law in employment discrimination is a section of the Civil Rights Act of 1964.

Under Title VII of the Civil Rights Act of 1964 it is unlawful to discriminate in employment on the basis of race. However, Title VII also contains a limitation aimed at not *requiring* any employer to grant preferential treatment to any group because of the race of such a group or because of any de facto racial imbalance in an employer's work force. In 1979 in *United Steelworkers v. Weber* a white employee, citing Title VII, challenged his employer's affirmative action training program.[27] The program had been arranged as a part of a collective-bargaining agreement in which the employer, Kaiser Aluminium, agreed to eliminate conspicuous racial imbalances in its craft work forces by reserving for black employees 50 percent of the openings in in-plant craft-training programs. The quota was to remain in force until such time as the percentage of blacks in a plant was equal to the percentage of blacks in the local labor force. When Kaiser selected black employees with less seniority than Weber, Weber sued under Title VII.

In upholding this private and voluntary program, the Supreme Court held that Title VII's limiting proviso was aimed only at programs that would *require* race-conscious affirmative actions plans, not at voluntary efforts. Since the intention of Title VII was to encourage unions and employers to end the last vestiges of racially discriminatory practices, the majority held that private and voluntary steps to hasten the elimination of these practices was not prohibited under the title.[28]

Unlike affirmative action programs in the private sector, public sector affirmative action programs can give rise to constitutional questions.

---

[27]*United Steelworkers v. Weber*, U.S., (1979).
[28]See also *Franks v. Bowman Transportation Company*, 424 U.S. 747 (1976), upholding retroactive grant seniority to black employees discriminated against by certain employer hiring practices.

In *Regents v. Bakke*, a medical school of the University of California had an affirmative action program which reserved 16 of its 100 annual admissions for disadvantaged minority students.[29] A white male applicant was denied admission even though his benchmark score of 549 out of 600 was well above the benchmark scores of a number of minority students admitted under the affirmative action program.[30] Like the *Weber* case, the *Bakke* case posed the difficult problem of "reverse discrimination." Had the facts in *Bakke* been somewhat different, e.g. had there been prior official acts of racial or ethnic discrimination in admitting students, then the *Green* rational would have supported some form of action by the university to correct its prior conduct. But *Bakke* did not have such a predicate. The medical school, like many other public and private professional schools, had embarked on a voluntary program designed to increase minority representation in the medical profession in California. The question, then, was whether Allan Bakke was forced to pay a part of the price of this voluntary state effort? In short, did the state unconstitutionally discriminate against Bakke on the basis of his race?

When the Court accepted jurisdiction in the *Bakke* case, it was undoubtedly aware that clear and unequivocal answers to the *Bakke* facts would be difficult. To have upheld such a program could have been construed as an endorsement of state discrimination against whites. In answer to this, one could have argued that previous race-discrimination cases had always involved invidious rather than benign acts by a majority against a minority. The *Bakke* case posed a new issue of a benign act intended to assist a minority. Of course, to minority applicants the program was benign, but to Allan Bakke it could hardly seem benign. The mere fact that prior cases of odious or invidious racial classifications had only been applied against a minority is hardly a justification for placing in the law a rule that would allow an individual to be discriminated against because of his or her membership in a dominant group. The language of the equal protection clause is specifically directed at the protection of individuals.

On the other hand, if the Court had struck down the program in unequivocal terms, it would have set in motion litigation that would have attacked all publicly sponsored affirmative action programs that did not have the *Brown*-type predicate of prior state discrimination. In practical terms it would have meant the end of racially and ethnically conscious affirmative action programs in state universities and colleges outside of the South and border states. A return to the status quo in professional school admissions would have meant a return to an essentially all-white student population in most professional schools. In short, there was little likelihood that the *Bakke* decision would be decided in clear and unequivocal terms, and it was not.

The Court was narrowly divided in the *Bakke* case, and the judgment was correspondingly narrow. A five-justice majority upheld the

---

[29]*Regents v. Bakke*, 98 S.Ct. 2733.
[30]The benchmark score was a composite score based on grade point averages, the MCAT score plus letters of recommendation, biographical data, and an interview summary.

California Supreme Court's ruling that the special admissions program violated the equal protection clause and, therefore, that Bakke had a right to be admitted to the School of Medicine. Justice Powell's opinion noted that the "purpose of helping certain groups whom the faculty . . . perceived to be victims of 'societal discrimination' does not justify a classification that imposes disadvantages upon persons like respondent [Bakke], who bear no responsibility for whatever harm the beneficiaries of the special admissions program are thought to have suffered."[31] On the other hand, the Court reversed the California holding that race could not be used in the admissions process. Instead, Justice Powell suggested that while a special admissions program focusing solely on race or ethnic background was not permitted, nonetheless, race or ethnic background could be *one* factor to be used in a program designed to encourage a diverse student body. Justice Powell argued that:

> In such an admissions program, race or ethnic background may be deemed a "plus" in a particular applicant's file, yet it does not insulate the individual from comparison with all other candidates for the available seats. The file of a particular black applicant may be examined for his potential contribution to diversity without the factor of race being decisive when compared, for example, with that of an applicant identified as an Italian-American if the latter is thought to exhibit qualities more likely to promote beneficial educational pluralism . . . exceptional personal talents, unique work or service experience, leadership potential, maturity, demonstrated compassion, a history of overcoming disadvantage, ability to communicate with the poor, or other qualifications deemed important.[32]

Of course, it could be argued that what Justice Powell was sanctioning was simply a shift from overt to covert racial and ethnic preferential treatment. The answer to this will have to await future action by the state universities that have previously used an exclusively racial/ethnic quota system for professional school admissions. What the *Bakke* decision may do is simply to drive underground what the universities were doing previously on an open basis. In any event, it is unlikely that the constitutional issues of racial and ethnic affirmative action programs generally can be resolved under the *Bakke* decision.

While the Court may be willing to require public universities to modify any exclusively racial/ethnic affirmative action programs, the Court faces a somewhat different problem in examining congressionally mandated race/ethnic-conscious affirmative action programs. For example, under a section of the Public Works Employment Act of 1977,[33] Congress mandated that local government recipients reserve at least 10 percent of the awarded funds for minority business enterprises. Thus, minority contractors were entitled to bid on 100 percent of the available funds and were assured of receiving at least 10 percent, whereas

[31]*Regents v. Bakke*, 98 S.Ct. 2759.
[32]Ibid., pp. 2762–2763.
[33]91 Stat. 116–121, P.L. No. 95-28.

white contractors could bid on only 90 percent of the available funds. The section specifically defined such enterprises as those enterprises in which there is at least 50 percent ownership by citizens who are Negroes, Spanish-speaking, Orientals, Indians, or Aleuts. The quota was not predicated on any specific finding of prior discrimination in the awarding of similar public works funds nor did it require that local agencies make such determination before the quota would become operative.

State-mandated racial quotas are not per se prohibited by the equal protection clause. They could pass the strict scrutiny test that applies to suspect classifications, such as race or alienage. The twofold test requires that the government demonstrate (1) a compelling state interest in using such a quota, and (2) that the quota is the least intrusive method of achieving this state interest. In the *Bakke* case as well as in the Public Works Employment Act of 1977, it is not too difficult to meet the requirement of a compelling state interest. The absence of minority contractors as well as the absence of minority doctors is the byproduct of a long history of educational and economic discrimination against minorities. Correcting this situation and ensuring social harmony is not only a legitimate but a compelling public responsibility. The second aspect of the strict scrutiny test, the least-intrusive-method requirement, was the principal problem in the *Bakke* case, and it would appear to be the major constitutional hurdle in the 10 percent set-aside provision. In *Bakke*, the Court concluded that there were alternatives available that could accomplish the objective with less intrusion into the rights of Allan Bakke. Whether Congress could devise a substitute affirmative action program that would encourage and promote minority business enterprises and be less intrusive than the 10 percent set-aside provision is an open question. In 1980 the Supreme Court upheld the 10 percent set-aside provision and noted that Congress has the power to try new techniques, including the limited use of racial and ethnic criteria, to accomplish remedial objectives.[34]

THE RIGHTS OF WOMEN

> He will hold thee, when his
> passion shall have spent
> its natural force,
> Something better than his dog,
> a little dearer than his horse.
> —*Alfred, Lord Tennyson,*
> *Locksley Hall, 1842*

One of the great blind spots in American constitutional history has been discrimination against women. While America has been slow to fulfill the promises of racial freedom, still the ideology of racial superiority has been long subject to challenge in scientific and moral arenas,[35]

[34]Fullilove v. Klutznick, ___ U.S. ___ (1980).
[35]For example, Ruth Benedict, *Race, Science and Politics*, Modern Age Books, New York, 1940.

and by the late 1930s scientific racism had been thoroughly debunked.[36] On the other hand, sexual discrimination, with deeper roots in Western history, has only recently become an acknowledged legal issue. For well over fifty years legal circles have been attempting to cope with racial discrimination; yet, except for the women's suffrage movement, the issue of the legal rights of women has been largely ignored. The discrimination was there, but it occupied the attention of practically no one in the male legal fraternity. An occasional bold woman would join issue with the law, but her efforts were usually unsuccessful and viewed as quarrelsome. The feminist revolt of the 1960s has, however, begun to make many Americans conscious of the legal consequences of hundreds of years of sexual stereotyping. Yet deeply embedded cultural perceptions, having found their way into statutory law and legal custom, cannot be erased in a decade. For generations women were perceived both by men and by themselves as emotionally and physically weak, incompetent in all matters outside of the home. Unable to think logically, they were passive but pure creatures, deserving of protection, yet essentially homemakers or decorative ornaments, romantic and charming playthings. In short, since she was more than a child and less than a man, a woman needed the protective cover of the law and, should she marry, the financial support and control of the strong, aggressive male. While all of this conjures up more an image of Dickens' Little Emily than it does of Betty Friedan, years of sexual stereotyping have had a tremendous and, on the whole, negative impact on the legal status of women in the United States. Indeed, although females have constituted a majority of our population since the late 1940s, their cultural and legal position in America conforms to the classic definition of a minority group as one singled out, by reason of a characteristic, for differential and unequal treatment.

Results of this differential and unequal treatment are everywhere. Although women were given equal voting rights in 1920, women are today vastly underrepresented in government and politics. Women do all kinds of low-level tasks in political campaigning, but they rarely run for a major public office let alone join the smoke-filled councils. In 1980, there was only one woman in the United States Senate, only two in the Cabinet, none on the Supreme Court, and only sixteen in the House of Representatives. There was only one female general in 1980 and no female admirals, and only three female mayors of major cities. However, women have made important political gains in the past decade. In 1974, Ella Grasso of Connecticut became the first woman elected governor in her own right. This was followed in 1976 by the election of Dixy Lee Ray as governor of Washington.

And in the economic arena the picture is not too different. Women own the majority of the corporate wealth of America, but they do not control it. While they may make it to the annual stockholders' meeting, they rarely make it into the board room. Of course, over 40 million American women are employed in the labor force, but their median income in 1979 was only approximately 36 percent of the income of working males. Indeed,

---

[36]See James W. Vander Zanden, "The Ideology of White Supremacy," *Journal of the History of Ideas*, vol. 20, pp. 385–402, 1959.

TABLE 4   Educational attainment and income by sex for persons 25 years and over, 1977

Four years of high school

	Male %	Female %
$ 1–$ 7,999	25.8	78.0
8,000– 9,999	12.1	10.6
10,000– 14,999	32.5	9.4
15,000– 24,999	25.4	2.7
25,000–and over	4.1	0.2

Four or more years of college

	Male %	Female %
$ 1–$ 7,999	15.1	47.8
8,000– 9,999	6.9	13.2
10,000– 14,999	21.1	25.8
15,000– 24,999	34.8	11.3
25,000–and over	22.1	1.7

Source: Compiled from National Center for Educational Statistics, *Digest of Educational Statistics*, 1977–78 ed., Government Printing Office, 1978, p. 182. This table does not control for part-time employment.

while the median school years completed by men and women is approximately the same, the correlation between income and educational attainment is much lower for women than for men, as seen in Table 4.

THE LEGAL ORDER AND WOMEN

> And Adam said, this is now bone of my bones, and flesh of my flesh: she shall be called Woman, because she was taken out of Man. Therefore shall a man leave his father and his mother, and shall cleave unto his wife: and they shall be one flesh.
>
> —*Genesis 2:23–24*

The consequences of sexual stereotyping have been evident not only in the economic and political order but also in the legal order. The protective domination of men led to the common-law assumption that through marriage the husband and wife become one, but as the late Justice Black noted, the "one" here is the husband.[37]

This common-law fiction was a result of the feudal doctrine of coverture, a doctrine that held that upon marriage women were legally subjugated to their husbands, particularly in respect to property rights. An attempt to redress this situation began in 1839 when Mississippi adopted

[37]Dissenting in *United States v. Yazell*, 382 U.S. 341, 361 (1966).

the first Married Women's Property Act. Similar acts were adopted in other states. The acts restored to married women the right to control and manage their own property. Over the years many of the remnants of male legal subjugation of wives have been discarded in favor of equal legal rights. But the legal system in some states is still not totally free of sex discrimination in property rights. For example, some common-law states still limit the wife's capacity to independently control her separate property; some restrict the right of married women to engage in business without prior approval of their husbands; still other restrictions limit the right of married women to dispose of their property freely, particularly in discharge of a husband's debt. On the other hand, community-property states, recognizing the limitations married women have faced in independently acquiring financial security, have accorded to each spouse an equal share of assets acquired after marriage. Yet even in some community-property states wives do not have equal control over the community property.

Beyond the issue of equal property rights, the common-law fiction that husband and wife are "one flesh" has greatly influenced the whole area of the law of domestic relations. By custom women, upon marrying surrender their maiden names; and their domicile for such purposes as voting and taxation is thereafter, in many states, determined by the domicile of the husband. Of course, the law of domestic relations has another side. The economic subordination of wives led the law to hold that the husband has a legal responsibility, enforceable by the criminal law in most states, to support his wife and children. And even though divorce is one of the most common legal transactions in modern America, there are still remnants of sex discrimination in laws governing divorce, alimony, and child custody.

Legal discrimination against women was a natural consequence of assigning women the limited roles of homemaker and mother and of assuming female inability to compete with men. However appropriate and even beneficial legislative classifications based on sex were in late Victorian society, they are largely an anachronism today. Justice Bradley observed in 1873 that "the civil law, as well as nature herself, has recognized a wide difference in the respective spheres and destinies of man and woman. Man is, or should be, woman's protector and defender. The natural and proper timidity and delicacy which belongs to the female sex evidently unfits it for many of the occupations of civil life."[38] This attitude of what was "natural and proper" led to the passage of legislation designed to protect women, such as protective labor legislation controlling rest and meal periods, minimum wages and maximum hours, night work, and the exclusion of women from dangerous or socially undesirable occupations. The same attitude led state legislatures and the Congress to assume that women were incapable of full participation in the civic life of the community and nation. They were exempted from draft laws, and as recently as the early 1970s a majority of the states gave women a full or partial exemption from jury service.[39]

[38]*Bradwell v. Illinois*, 83 U.S. 130, 141 (1873).
[39]In *Taylor v. Louisiana*, 95 S.Ct. 692 (1975), the Supreme Court struck down a statute that effectively gave women a blanket exemption from jury service, thereby casting constitutional doubt on similar legislation in other jurisdictions.

SEX AS A LEGAL CLASSIFICATION

Doubtless much of the early protecting and exempting legislation, while clearly intended to make discrimination legal, was not intended to work to a woman's disadvantage. Legislation must frequently classify persons simply in order to define the scope of prohibitions, exemptions, and benefits due them. Legislative classification of persons by certain statutorily defined characterisitics is common to many forms of legislation, such as tax law, social security legislation, education law, and labor legislation. Classification of persons by sex also has been a common feature of many laws, and when constitutional doubts were first raised about the legality of such sex-based distinctions, lower courts could for many years point to a Supreme Court decision which tacitly recognized the appropriateness of sexual classification. At the turn of the century Oregon, as a part of the progressive movement, passed an act limiting the hours women, but not men, could work in factories. The intent was not only to protect women against sweat-labor shops, but probably to open the door generally to protective labor legislation. The Supreme Court, aided by an able brief by a future Supreme Court justice, Louis D. Brandeis, upheld the Oregon law. Incorporating Brandeis' argument, the Court reasoned as follows:

> That woman's physical structure and the performance of maternal functions place her at a disadvantage in the struggle for subsistence is obvious. This is especially true when the burdens of motherhood are upon her. . . . Still again, history discloses the fact that woman has always been dependent upon man. He established his control at the outset by superior physical strength, and this control in various forms, with diminishing intensity, has continued to the present. . . . [I]n the struggle for subsistence she is not an equal competitor with her brother. . . . [T]here is that in her disposition and habits of life which will operate against a full assertion of those rights. She will still be where some legislation to protect her seems necessary to secure a real equality of right. . . . Differentiated by these matters from the other sex, she is properly placed in a class by herself, and legislation designed for her protection may be sustained, even when like legislation is not necessary for men, and could not be sustained. It is impossible to close one's eye to the fact that she still looks to her brother and depends upon him. Even though all restrictions on political, personal, and contractual rights were taken away, and she stood, so far as statutes are concerned, upon an absolutely equal plane with him, it would still be true that she is so constituted that she will rest upon and look to him for protection; that her physical structure and a proper discharge of her maternal functions . . . justify legislation to protect her from the greed as well as the passion of man.[40]

Only three years before the *Muller* case the Court had struck down a New York law limiting the number of hours individuals could work in bakeries.[41] While the Oregon law was upheld, the Court returned to its so-called freedom of contract position in 1923, when it again struck

[40]*Muller v. Oregon*, 208 U.S. 412, 421–422 (1908).
[41]*Lochner v. New York*, 198 U.S. 45 (1905).

down legislation to protect labor, this time a congressional act establishing minimum wages for women and children in the District of Columbia.[42] Thus the *Muller* case, given the legal current running against it, offered some faint hope that the door had been slightly opened to legislation protecting labor. The irony of the *Muller* case was that years later it would be cited by those who wished to lock women out of the labor movement. This happened when protecting and exempting legislation became a mechanism in the Depression of the 1930s for excluding women from the labor market. As social and economic conditions altered, and advantages turned into liabilities, many women raised constitutional arguments against sex-based classification.

The major constitutional argument against sex-based classification has focused on the equal protection of the laws clause of the Fourteenth Amendment. This clause has been variously used for attacking a variety of legislative classifications, and over the years the Supreme Court has designed two tests to be applied to classifications. One test is called the strict judicial scrutiny test and has been applied to classifications that are inherently suspect, such as race[43] or national origin,[44] and classification dealing with a fundamental interest, such as the right to vote[45] or the right to interstate travel.[46] Classifications subject to strict judicial scrutiny will be held invalid in the absence of a compelling governmental interest. The second test, covering all other circumstances, is less onerous and simply requires that the classifications not be patently arbitrary and that they have a reasonable relationship to a legitimate governmental interest.[47]

The second or traditional test has been generally applied by courts to sex-based classification. In 1948 the Supreme Court upheld a Michigan statute forbidding women from being licensed as bartenders, except the wives and daughters of owners of liquor establishments. The majority concluded that the law was a reasonable regulation of a social problem. In dissent three justices called the classification an invidious and arbitrary distinction and as such a denial to women of the equal protection of the law.[48] More recently courts have been pressed to hold that sex is a suspect classification and as such is subject to the strict judicial scrutiny test. In 1971 the Supreme Court rejected an opportunity to do this. It did rule that an Idaho law that provided that, as between persons equally qualified to administer estates, males were to be preferred to females, was a denial of equal protection of the laws to females.[49] Two years later the Court again was confronted with a sex-based classification, this time a federal law controlling benefit allowances for military dependents. The statute provided that spouses of male members of the armed forces were dependents for purposes of obtaining

[42]*Adkins v. Children's Hospital*, 261 U.S. 525 (1923).
[43]For example, *Loving v. Virginia*, 388 U.S. 1 (1967).
[44]For example, *Oyama v. California*, 332 U.S. 633 (1948).
[45]For example, *Dunn v. Blumstein*, 405 U.S. 330 (1972).
[46]For example, *Shapiro v. Thompson*, 394 U.S. 618 (1969).
[47]For example, *Morey v. Doud*, 354 U.S. 457 (1957).
[48]See *Goēsaert v. Cleary*, 335 U.S. 464 (1948).
[49]*Reed v. Reed*, 404 U.S. 71 (1971).

increased allowances for quarters and for medical and dental benefits. However, the statute said that spouses of female members of the armed services were not dependents unless in fact they obtained over half of their support from their wives. In effect a discriminatory need formula was being used against female members of the armed services.[50] With only Justice Rehnquist dissenting, the Court struck down the provision as a violation of the due process clause.[51] However, the majority could not agree on a single opinion. The plurality opinion of Justice Brennan joined by Justices Douglas, White, and Marshall, concluded that sex was a suspect classification, reasoning that:

> . . . since sex, like race and national origin, is an immutable characteristic determined solely by the accident of birth, the imposition of special disabilities upon the members of a particular sex because of their sex, would seem to violate the basic concept of our system, that legal burdens should bear some relationship to individual responsibility. . . . And what differentiates sex from such non-suspect statutes as intelligence or physical disability, and aligns it with recognized suspect criteria, is that the sex characteristic frequently bears no relation to ability to perform or contribute.[52]

Applying the strict judicial scrutiny test the plurality found that the differential treatment was merely a matter of administrative convenience. Convenience alone was not a sufficient or compelling governmental interest, particularly since there was "substantial evidence that if put to the test, many of the wives of male members would fail to qualify for benefits."[53]

While the Court has refused to denote sex as a suspect classification, a majority of the justices appear to regard gender classifications as subject to a more rigorous examination than obtains under the rational basis test. The Court noted in 1977 that gender-based classifications must serve an important governmental objective and that the classification must be substantially related to achieving such an objective.[54] One such legislative objective that the Court has approved is the reduction in the disparity in the economic condition between men and women or the compensation of women for prior economic discrimination. Thus in *Califano v. Webster*, the Court upheld a challenged

---

[50]*Frontiero v. Richardson*, 93 S.Ct. 1764 (1973); discriminating dependency formulas can also work against males, and in *Califano v. Goldfarb*, 97 S.Ct. 1021 (1977) the Court struck down a Social Security provision that allowed widows to receive benefits without proof of dependency whereas a widower was entitled to the same benefit only upon proof that he had received at least half of his support from his spouse. The plurality opinion noted that such a dependency theory rested on an archaic and overbroad generalization.

[51]In federal cases the due process clause of the Fifth Amendment is the functional equivalent of the equal protection clause, the latter applying only to state action.

[52]*Frontiero v. Richardson*, 93 S.Ct. 1770 (1973).

[53]Ibid., p. 1772. Administrative convenience was also disallowed in the blanket exclusion of women from jury service. "It is untenable to suggest these days that it would be a special hardship for each and every woman to perform jury service or that society cannot spare any women from their present duties." *Taylor v. Louisiana*, 95 S.Ct. 692 (1975).

[54]*Califano v. Webster*, 97 S.Ct. 1192, 1194 (1977).

Social Security provision even though the provision allowed women a greater advantage than men in computing retirement benefits. While Congress subsequently repealed the favorable benefit computation for women, the Court agreed that the benefit had been conferred on women to compensate for prior economic disabilities.[55] Similarly, the Court has upheld a federal provision that allows women line naval officers an advantage over male line officers in situations governing mandatory discharge.[56] The Court agreed that the advantage was not unconstitutional since it was conferred in compensation for the lack of opportunity for professional advancement occasioned by restrictions on female line officers participating in combat duty and most sea duty.

Similarly in *Kahn v. Shevin*, a majority of the Court upheld a Florida annual $500 property tax exemption for widows against a challenge that it denied a widower the equal protection of Florida laws.[57] The majority reasoned that while the law discriminated on the basis of gender, it rested on a reasonable distinction in state policy, namely, to cushion the financial impact of spousal loss that is disproportionately experienced by widows. It is difficult to reconcile the *Kahn* decision with other cases in which the Court has struck down gender classifications that are predicated on an economic dependency assumption. Thus, in *Califano v. Wescott*, the Court disallowed a provision in Social Security legislation that extended benefits to families with dependent children where the father was unemployed, but did not extend any benefit when the mother was unemployed.[58] The majority concluded that this gender classification rested on no important governmental objective but rather on the baggage of sexual stereotypes that assume that the male has the primary responsibility for providing a home.[59] Indeed, in recent years the Court has struck down numerous laws that are based on sexual stereotyping. For example, in an Alabama divorce case involving a law that allowed only wives to receive alimony, the majority indicated that sex cannot be used as a proxy for financial need.[60] The Court noted that "Legislative classifications which distribute benefits and burdens on the basis of gender carry the inherent risk of reinforcing the stereotypes about the 'proper place' of women and their need for special protection. Thus, even statutes purportedly designed to compensate for and ameliorate the effects of past discrimination, must be carefully tailored. Where, as here, the state's compensatory and ameliorative purposes are as well served by a gender-neutral classification as one that gender-classifies and therefore carries with it the baggage of sexual stereotypes, the state cannot be permitted to classify on the basis of sex."[61] And in a Utah case the Court overturned a child support law that provided that girls attained their majority at age eighteen (and hence

[55]Ibid., p. 1196.
[56]*Schlesinger v. Ballard*, 95 S.Ct. 572 (1975).
[57]*Kahn v. Shevin*, 416 U.S. 351 (1974).
[58]*Califano v. Wescott*, 99 S.Ct. 2655 (1979).
[59]See also *Califano v. Goldfarb*, 97 S.Ct. 1021 (1977).
[60]*Orr v. Orr*, 99 S.Ct. 1102 (1979).
[61]Ibid., p. 113.

were no longer eligible for child support) whereas boys attained their majority at age twenty-one.[62] In striking down the Utah provision, the Court noted that "If a specified age of minority is required for the boy in order to assure him parental support while he attains his education and training, so, too, is it for the girl. To distinguish between the two on educational grounds is to be self-serving: if the female is not to be supported so long as the male, she hardly can be expected to attend school as long as he does, and bringing her education to an end earlier coincides with the role-typing society has long imposed."[63]

Even gender classifications which appear to rest on some objective difference have come under close examination. Thus in a California case, female public employees were required to contribute to the pension fund at a slightly higher rate than male employees. The differential rested on the objective fact that females live longer and, thus, would presumably enjoy greater benefits.[64] The Court ruled that such a distinction, nonetheless, unfairly discriminated against those females who will not live as long as the average male and, therefore, violates Title VII of the Civil Rights Act of 1964.[65]

With few exceptions, the decisions of the Supreme Court have been moving in the direction of disallowing legislation that role-types females as dependents or as homemakers and that use sex as a proxy for need. Since several important areas of law—domestic relations and welfare law, for example—have often proceeded on the basis of a dependency theory of women, it will take some time to make the adjustments necessary to sexual equality. In the meantime, it may be necessary to allow a degree of differential treatment, particularly for older women, in order to compensate for prior economic discrimination. The danger in allowing differential treatment is that it may perpetuate the stereotypes that initially gave rise to the economic discriminations.

PREGNANCY AND THE LAW

A further illustration of the inequities of sex-based classifications can be seen in the area of governmental regulations pertaining to pregnancy. School boards, and other agencies, have commonly imposed uniform mandatory unpaid maternity leaves for pregnant teachers. In 1974 the Supreme Court struck down two such regulations that imposed an arbitrary termination well in advance of the expected date of birth. The Court ruled that such arbitrary cutoff dates created a conclusive presumption that a pregnant teacher is physically incapable of continuing her duties and thus violated the due process clause. In the two cases decided in 1974 the mandatory termination provisions were set at the fourth and fifth months of pregnancy.[66]

Although such arbitrary maternity leaves were struck down, the Court was unwilling to hold a state disability insurance program that excluded

[62]*Stanton v. Stanton*, 421 U.S. 7 (1975).

[63]Ibid., p. 15; see also *Craig v. Boren*, 97 S.Ct. 451 (1976).

[64]*City of Los Angeles v. Manhart*, 98 S.Ct. 1370 (1978).

[65]Cf. *Personnel Administrative Review of Massachusetts v. Fenney*, 99 S.Ct. 2282 (1979).

[66]*Cleveland Board of Education v. LaFleur*, 94 S.Ct. 791 (1974).

pregnancy as violative of the equal protection clause. Under a California program women disabled from work due to normal pregnancy are ineligible for disability insurance. The Court upheld this exclusion and concluded that the classification was not an invidious discrimination because a state is not required to attack every aspect of a social problem but may draw a line that is rationally supportable.[67] The Court found a rational basis for the exclusion in that if pregnancy were included, the present fiscal viability of the program would be undermined.

The Court's rationale is not likely to convince the female employee who has contributed to the program and whose normal pregnancy is medically disabling. Arbitrary discriminations may frequently have an underlying fiscal rationale; yet that should not exempt the classifications from close judicial scrutiny, particularly where the classification is sex-based. The Court has given some indication that it will closely examine how private employers treat pregnancy in the context of employee rights. Thus, in *Nashville Gas Company v. Satty*, the Court held that a private employer had violated Title VII of the Civil Rights Act of 1964 when it denied an employee returning from pregnancy leave the employee's accumulated seniority.[68] The Court ruled that by allowing *all* employees to retain accumulated seniority while on leave for nonoccupational disabilities other than pregnancy, the employer had imposed on women a substantial burden that men need not suffer.

Congress has also, on occasion, amended sexual classifications of a few federal programs. For example, in 1972 Congress amended a provision of the law governing benefits for dependents of veterans to read as follows: "For purposes of this title the term 'wife' includes husband of any female veteran and the term 'widow' includes the widower of any female veteran."[69] While not a particularly elegant phrase, the above does accomplish the objective of according equal treatment.

A good deal more legislative revision will be necessary in order to eliminate sex discrimination in the actions of government. A 1973 federal district court decision is illustrative of the problem. A three-judge New Jersey federal district court ruled that a 1939 provision of the Social Security Act allowing widows to qualify for a "mother's benefit" but not allowing widowers to qualify for a similar benefit denied equal protection not only to the widower but also to female wage-earners who are principal breadwinners for their families.[70] However logical it may have been in the 1930s to design social welfare programs based on certain assumptions about sexual roles, the economy of the 1980s defies such easy classification.

CONCLUSION

If individuals are indeed considered to be equal before the law inequities will have to be eliminated. A few of these legal inequities have been

[67]*Geduldig v. Aiello*, 94 S.Ct. 2485 (1974); reaffirmed in *General Electric Company v. Gilbert*, a Title VII, Civil Rights Act of 1964 case, ruling in support of the exclusion of pregnancy-related illness from a company's sickness benefit plan, 429 U.S. 125 (1976).

[68]*Nashville Gas Company v. Satty*, 98 S.Ct. 347 (1977).

[69]38 U.S.C. 103, 86 Stat. 1074.

[70]*Wiesenfeld v. Secretary of H. E. W.*, 367 F. Supp. 981 (1973), unanimously upheld by the Supreme Court in *Weinberger v. Wiesenfeld*, 95 S.Ct. (1975).

highlighted above. There is, of course, a long list of legal issues to be confronted. Change will not be easy. Surrendering deeply ingrained attitudes will evoke the passions of many. Yet the goal of full legal emancipation of women is a policy aimed not only at ending discrimination against women but also at enlarging everyone's freedom.

THE EQUAL RIGHTS AMENDMENT

It is unlikely that a majority of the Court will rule that sex is a suspect classification until there is some final resolution of the Equal Rights Amendment. The proposed amendment was adopted by Congress in March of 1972 and submitted to the states for ratification. The proposal, if adopted, provides that "equality of rights under the law shall not be denied or abridged by the United States or any State on account of sex." Presumably this provision would necessarily place sexual classifications in the suspect category. The great advantage of the proposed amendment is that it has the potential for sweeping away all vestiges of sexually discriminatory public policy—local, state, and federal. On the other hand, the very sweeping nature of the amendment is a source of some concern. Sex-based classifications are still common to many areas of public policy. A careful study and revision of individual statutes by legislative bodies might have been a preferable course of action.

Congress, of course, has made some effort to ensure equal treatment for women by providing in Title VII of the Civil Rights Act of 1964 that no one covered by employment provision of the act shall be discriminated against on the basis of sex. Similarly the Equal Pay Act of 1963 prohibits discrimination on the basis of sex. And the executive branch of the federal government has also attempted to eliminate sex discrimination in employment through the Office of Federal Contract Compliance. Under the OFCC all federal contractors and all contractors working on a federally assisted construction project must agree to an employment policy that does not discriminate on the basis of the race, color, religion, sex, or national origin of applicants and employees, and contractors must also agree to undertake a program of affirmative action to improve the representation of underutilized minorities.

Oh who is that young sinner with the handcuffs on his wrists?
And what has he been after that they groan and shake their fists?
And wherefore is he wearing such a conscience-stricken air?
Oh they're taking him to prison for the colour of his hair.

A. E. Houseman,
—Additional Poems #18

GAY RIGHTS

Homosexuals long have been the subject of social condemnation and a hostile legal system. Whatever may have been the level of sexual tolerance in ancient Greece, the cultures and legal systems of Judeo-Christian societies generally have been harsh and brutal in treating homosexuals. While this legacy is being challenged today, still the challenge must surmount anti-homosexual convictions, convictions that often rest on strong religious beliefs. Yet merely because society has condemned homosexuality as immoral, it does not follow that homosexuals are condemned by the Constitution. The Constitution does not exclude any person from its protection or consign any person to outer darkness. Yet by assigning the criminal label to homosexual conduct, the state often has effectively condemned large numbers of individuals to a truncated and furtive life.

CRIMINALIZATION OF
HOMOSEXUAL CONDUCT

As of 1979, twenty-nine states had statutes prohibiting "deviant" sexual behavior.[71] All of these statutes can be applied to private, consensual adult homosexual acts, and some of the states direct their so-called sodomy laws only at homosexual acts.[72] While prosecutions under these laws are uncommon, nonetheless, the laws are not without consequence. The very existence of such laws give reinforcement to both private and public acts of discrimination against homosexuals, especially in the area of employment. Furthermore, such laws raise important constitutional issues that both federal and state courts have long avoided. Public attitudes toward homosexual behavior, however, appear to be changing in the direction of greater tolerance. A 1977 Gallup Poll reported that Americans were equally divided in supporting and opposing laws legalizing adult homosexual relations.[73] Certainly during the 1970s, state legislatures were more receptive to legislation guaranteeing gay rights than during any previous era in America. While sound arguments can be made for focusing on legislative rather than judicial initiatives in reforming laws in this area, still the judiciary does have a responsibility to ensure that no person is denied due process or the equal protection of the laws.

SUBSTANTIVE DUE PROCESS AND
PRIVACY

In recent years the Supreme Court has recognized a constitutional right to privacy and in 1965 specifically applied it to the right of married couples to use contraceptives.[74] While in the 1965 case, the majority did not agree on the constitutional basis for this marital right of privacy, concurring opinions by Justices Harlan and White both rested on due

---

[71]For a listing of states, see Rhonda Rivera, "The Legal Position of Homosexuals in The United States," *Hastings Law Journal*, vol. 30, pp. 799, 949, 1979; however, during the 1970s a large number of states did decriminalize adult consensual private homosexual acts; see listing in ibid. pp. 950–951.

[72]For example, Montanna Rev. Codie Ann. 94-5-505.

[73]*Gallup Opinion Index*, no. 147, October 1977.

[74]*Griswold v. Connecticut*, 381 U.S. 479 (1965).

process arguments.[75] Subsequently, the Court extended this right to single individuals as well as married couples, noting that "If the right of privacy means anything, it is the right of the *individual*, married or single, to be free from unwarranted governmental intrusion into matters so fundamentally affecting a person as the decision whether to bear or beget a child."[76] Finally, in *Roe v. Wade*, the 1973 abortion decision, the Court noted that while the Constitution does not explicitly mention a right to privacy,

> In a line of decisions . . . the Court has recognized that a right of personal privacy, or a guarantee of certain areas or zones of privacy, does exist under the Constitution. . . . This right of privacy, whether it be founded in the Fourteenth Amendment's concept of personal liberty and restrictions upon state action, as we feel it is, or, as the District Court determined, in the Ninth Amendment's reservation of rights to the people, is broad enough to encompass a woman's decision whether or not to terminate her pregnancy.[77]

If the zone of personal privacy encompasses a decision to terminate pregnancy, by analogy it would seem plausible to maintain that it extends equally to adult consensual sexual and affectional preferences. Surely the adult decision to enter freely into a sexual relationship is the kind of very private decision that ought to preclude governmental intrusion unless there is a compelling state interest that would justify the intrusion.[78] Several state interests might be offered in justification for an intrusion into homosexual relations, among them:

1 The protection against sexual coercion, especially in the form of child molestation

2 Prevention and control of venereal disease

3 The preservation of public morality

4 The preservation of the institution of heterosexual marriage

Clearly, sexual coercion, whether by the heterosexual or the homosexual, is an important interest that requires a degree of state interest. Yet there is little evidence to support the contention that by treating private consensual *adult* homosexual behavior as criminal, a society will advance its interest in reducing the incidence of sexual violence. Society has a legitimate interest in retaining laws against sexual violence in any form, including, of course, coercive sexual conduct by homosexuals. However, there is the possibility that the criminalization of homosexual behavior may actually contribute to sexual violence by precluding a legal outlet for homosexual conduct. In any event, there

---

[75]Ibid., pp. 499–502; however, Justice Harlan's dissenting opinion in *Poe v. Ullman* specifically rejected homosexual conduct as a fundamental right protected by due process, 367 U.S. 497 (1961).

[76]*Eisenstadt v. Baird*, 405 U.S. 438, 452 (1972).

[77]*Roe v. Wade*, 410 U.S. 113, 152–153.

[78]The format that is being used in the following argument is generally used in equal-protection-of-the-law litigation. This so-called strict-scrutiny test may be appropriately applied to due process arguments.

appears to be little correlation between homosexual conduct and sexual violence.[79]

The prevention of venereal disease has long been a social interest that has justified state concern. Furthermore, there is a high incidence of venereal disease among male homosexuals. Yet there is something circular in this justification for a state intrusion. Criminal laws against homosexual conduct may well contribute to furtive and promiscuous sexual relations rather than stable relations. In turn, this may encourage male homosexual prostitution, the greatest source of the disease. The state's interest in preventing the spread of venereal disease can surely be accomplished by means less intrusive and more efficacious than sodomy laws.

There is little evidence to support the proposition that the threat of the criminal sanction acts as a deterrent to those who would engage in homosexual behavior. From a purely utilitarian point of view, it is questionable whether respect for morality is advanced by sanctions that have little impact on behavior. Furthermore, the logistical problems of enforcing laws against private consensual behavior can lead to police practices that militate against respect for the law. Finally, it is a dubious proposition to assert that the protection of public morality requires the imposition of the criminal sanction. The greatest deterrent to homosexual behavior is social stigma, and removing the criminal sanctions probably would not be interpreted by the public as an endorsement of homosexual behavior.[80]

The final argument in support of a compelling state interest in retaining the criminal sanction for homosexual conduct is that it advances the institution of marriage and traditional family life. The traditions of the family and heterosexual marriage have certainly been under assault; yet it is doubtful whether sodomy laws or laws against adultery or fornication have had any beneficial effect on preserving these institutions. There is probably a far greater correlation with the advent of working mothers and the breakdown of traditional family life than with homosexual behavior. Yet few would suggest that the state's interest here would justify making it a criminal offense for mothers or fathers to be absent from the home. The state's interest in preserving marriage as a heterosexual institution may well justify refusing to allow homosexuals to marry.[81] On the other hand, it does not necessarily follow that heterosexual marriage is encouraged by the mere existence of sodomy laws.

CONCLUSION

Of all of the problems in the area of gay rights, the problem of sodomy laws may be the least important. The laws are rarely enforced against

---

[79]See Note, "The Constitutionality of Laws Forbidding Private Homosexual Conduct," *Michigan Law Review*, vol. 72, pp. 1613–1630, (1974).
[80]See Herbert Packer, *The Limits of the Criminal Sanction*, Stanford University Press, Stanford, Calif., 1968, chap. 16.
[81]See for example, *Baker v. Nelson*, 191 N.W.2d 185 (1971), where the Minnesota Supreme Court ruled that the prohibition of same-sex marriage did not violate the right of privacy.

private consensual adult homosexual behavior. Yet the test of their importance cannot be measured solely by the degree of police enforcement. If sexual preference is a zone of privacy that merits constitutional protection, then the states should repeal their sodomy laws or the courts should strike them down. Furthermore, the very existence of such laws reinforces discrimination in housing and employment.[82] Finally, the existence of such laws may contribute to perpetuating homosexuality as a deviant subculture, hardly a goal that a constitutional order should encourage.

[82]See Joel Friedman, "Discrimination in Employment Based on Sexual Orientation," *Iowa Law Review*, vol. 64, p. 527, 1979.

2 FREEDOM OF THE PRESS

Freedom of the press is predicated at once on the requirements of the democratic process as well as on one of the fundamental goals of freedom, namely, the enhancement of the human personality. Without the political, economic, and social knowledge that can be gained through a free press, voters, public officials, and consumers often would be unable to make either meaningful or wise choices. In short, democracy assumes a level of public and private information that could only partially be obtained in the absence of a free and generally private press. The constant flow of information that comes out of radio, television, newspapers, books, and periodicals, some profound and some trivial, is essential to freedom of choice. Furthermore, a free press is an important outlet for self-expression not only in politics but also in literature and the arts. Thus, a free press can be a stabilizing force in society to the extent that it provides an outlet for the orderly challenging of the status quo and for individual self-fulfillment.

Like all freedoms, a free press is sometimes a mixed blessing. For example, the freedom to publish carries with it a certain license to curry the public's favor, and even to pander to interests and curiosities that span the human condition, serving at once the banal and morbid as well as the profound needs of humankind.

Beyond our frequent concern about a sometimes artless and shameless press, we must also direct our attention to the conflict that is created by the search for information. A vigorous and competitive press has a great appetite for information. The search for information may lead the press into areas that some think are beyond the zone of freedom or it may lead the press to attempt to draw a wider zone of freedom simply in order to protect itself from governmental intrusion. In short, freedom of the press is the beginning point in an inquiry rather than the end. The Constitution sets forth a principle to be followed, not a set of boundaries. One boundary line involves pre- and post-publication censorship of obscene printed matter.

CENSORSHIP IN HISTORY

Censorship by governmental authority can be traced back to Greek and Roman societies and on into early church history. Early censorship by church and state was directed primarily at heresy and political attacks on the state rather than obscenity. The phenomenon of widespread censorship of obscenity was a product of modern technology and its consequent mass culture. Modern technology began with Caxton's introduction of the printing press in England in 1476. The next two centuries witnessed a growing concern about the problem of public morals and obscene books. Still the principal concern of both church and state was over the influence that an uncontrolled press might have in politics and theology.

Defense of a free press   While political and religious censorship continued intermittently throughout the sixteenth and seventeenth centuries there was a growing opposition to governmental interference with the press. The best-known and most widely quoted defense of a free press was made by John Milton in his *Areopagitica* in 1644, and practical arguments offered against censorship today are largely the same arguments that Milton presented more than three hundred years ago. Now, as then, the argument begins with the assumption that man is a free creature with the ability to make reasonable choices. Free men must have the right to seek the truth. They must have "the liberty to know, to utter, and to argue freely according to conscience."

Perhaps the greatest appeal today for Milton's treatise is his practical defense of the freedom to read. Milton posed the question that the defenders of a free press have asked in all subsequent generations: "How shall the licensers themselves be confided in, unless we can confer upon them, or they assume to themselves above all others in the land, the grace of infallibility and uncorruptedness?" More recent critics of censorship were less charitable when they noted that the case for censorship must stand or fall on its being administered by the wisest man in the world. "But no wise man would accept such a post. As things are constituted it is pretty safe to assume that any given censor is a fool. The very fact that he is a censor indicates that."[1]

Puritanism   For many years a favorite theme of critics of censorship has been that the healthy attitude toward sex that had existed in literature was suddenly changed by a group of sour-faced Puritans bent upon making everybody as miserable as possible. There is some truth and a considerable amount of fiction in such a proposition. The dour and self-righteous Puritan that people think of today is largely the product of the cartoonists. It is true that the Puritans were concerned with a reformation in manners; they did tend to emphasize piety and chastity; and they did expect one's life to be directed to the glory of God. They were not opposed to pleasure and certainly not opposed to sex. About all that can be legitimately ascribed to Puritans in this area is an influence on later legal developments. But they bequeathed a heritage of squeamishness of speech and action upon which the neo-Calvinists in the eighteenth century embellished and enlarged.

[1]Heywood Broun and Margaret Leach, *Anthony Comstock: Roundsman of the Lord*, Literary Guild, New York. 1927. p 275

The Restoration Few periods in literary history have been totally free of earthy literature. Chaucer wrote "The Miller's Tale" and Shakespeare is still known to many as the bawdy bard. Of course, Chaucer also wrote romances for knightly circles and Shakespeare is also remembered as the Biblical bard. Still, some periods appear to have been freer in sex expression in literature than others. The Restoration was such a period.

Hippolyte Taine said, with quaint bluntness that when we pass from the noble portraits of Van Dyck in the reign of Charles I to the figures of Peter Lely in the reign of Charles II, "we have left a palace and lighted on a bagnio.[2]" Much of the Restoration verse and drama stands out as sensual and bawdy. It seems that the Earl of Rochester set out to bury heroic love and came close to doing just that with his bawdy verses. The foes of contemporary sex censorship delight in informing their readers that the present censorship of obscenity is really a ridiculous denial of the earthy robustness of our literary history, particularly as it is exemplified by the Restoration period. Certainly Restoration drama does afford abundant opportunity to stress the acceptance of sex as a legitimate tool in literary style. But the fact remains that what is termed erotic realism today is not some unbroken heritage of the past. Dryden and Rochester abound in erotica, but this simply reflects a basic aristocratic cynicism in morals and manners, a reaction to the interlude of Puritans, rather than an acceptance of obscenity. Finally, the uninhibited works of the court wits were not written for mass audiences but rather for the aristocracy, a fact that most opponents of obscenity censorship ignore.

The eighteenth century It was not until the eighteenth century that a literary reading public emerged in England and the American colonies. Two seemingly contradictory developments occurred concurrently with the emergence of this new reading public: an increasing sensitiveness on the part of the government to the circulation of allegedly obscene printed matter, and a general acceptance of the broad principle of freedom of the press.

It is not surprising that with the increased circulation of the press there was also an increase in the volume of obscene books and a resultant concern over their distribution. A Scottish minister wrote in the first quarter of the eighteenth century that "all the villanous profane and obscene books and plays printed at London by Curle and other are gote doun from London by Allan Ramsey, and lent out, for an easy price, to young boyes, servant weemen of the better sort and gentlemen, and vice and obscenity dreadfully propagated."[3]

What the minister was witnessing was the rise of the lending or circulating library. This institution was made possible in the early eighteenth century by the availability of cheap paper and a rising urban population. Gradually, the governing class became alarmed over the social prob-

---

[2]Hippolyte Taine, *History of English Literature*, 2d ed. Edmonston and Douglas, Edinburgh, 1872, vol. 1. p. 458.
[3]Robert Wodrow, *Analecta; or, Materials for a History of Remarkable Providences*, Edinburgh Print Company, Edinburgh, 1843, vol. III, p. 515.

lems that they expected to result from this new freedom in reading. Curl, the lending librarian spoken of by the Scottish minister, was in fact the first person convicted in an English secular court for publishing an obscene book. The title of the book was *Venus in the Cloister*, or, *The Nun in Her Smock*. The case, which was decided in 1727, marked a fundamental change in English law.[4] Only a few years before the *Curl* case the courts had refused to accept jurisdiction in a similar case.[5] After the *Curl* case, it was accepted that obscene publications could be restrained.

Nonetheless, freedom of the press was gradually accepted as a principle of American and English government at the same time that government censorship of obscenity was occuring with increased regularity. The most celebrated American case was tried in New York in 1734. Peter Zenger was arrested on a charge of seditious libel, accused of printing a political attack on the governor. At that time in England and in the Colonies, seditious libel was not defined by any law; and hence a man did not know in advance whether his publications would offend those in authority or not. The heart of the matter was that while the defendant was tried before a jury, the jury was not allowed to decide whether in fact the book or paper was libelous. In the *Zenger* case, the court ruled that the defense could not introduce evidence to prove the truth of Zenger's statements and further that the court, and not the jury, would determine whether the statements were libelous. The jury refused to convict Zenger. The result of this case was that the people had asserted a new authority over the government's attempt to control the press,

Throughout the remainder of the eighteenth century the principle of freedom of the press gained further acceptance. In 1776, the Virginia Bill of Rights was adopted, and it included a statement that the "freedom of the press is one of the great bulwarks of liberty, and can never be restrained but by despotick governments." When the federal Bill of Rights was adopted in 1791, it included a restriction in the First Amendment against the federal abridgment of a free press: "Congress shall make no law . . . abridging the freedom . . . of the press."

While freedom of the press was gaining recognition as an operating principle of government, few believed that the principle was absolute. There was general acceptance of the rule that the government was precluded from prior restraint, that is, prepublication censorship of the press. The great eighteenth-century legal commentator, Sir William Blackstone, wrote: "The liberty of the press is indeed essential to the nature of a free state; but this consists in laying no previous restraints upon publications, and not in freedom from censure for criminal matter when published." Thus, while the law of libel was considerably narrowed in the late eighteenth century, it has remained a legitimate means of punishing the malicious defamation of a person by publications. Similarly, the publication of obscenity was not considered immune from governmental restraint.

[4]*Rex v Curl*, 2 Stra. 783 (1727).
[5]*Queen v. Read,* 11 Mod. 142 (1703).

THE VICTORIAN CONSCIENCE

With the advent of the industrial revolution, first in England and later in the United States, literary taste underwent a vast transformation. Sometime in the late eighteenth century the novel became dainty, and sex was all but banished from the reading matter offered to the public.

The prelude to what we today call the Victorian conscience started in the 1780s with the evangelical movement. The rising middle class had more leisure time for reading, and the evangelicals set about substituting "good" reading matter for "bad." A new moral orthodoxy was introduced. Novels had to have a moral purpose; and, more importantly, they had to be "proper" companions for women and children. As the drawing room became the center of the middle-class family, books had to be sufficiently decorous to lie on the drawing-room table without offending the eyes of a young lady. The book became a symbol of refinement and taste.[6]

In fairness to the evangelicals and the early Victorians, it must be said that they were reacting to new social and moral problems, problems that were the by-products of the industrial revolution and the urban movement. There was an increasing market for pornography—from the highly priced erotica designed for the bibliophiles to the vulgar trash designed for the mass public. In a limited way, then, the new conscience was a means of self-defense.

Unfortunately the evangelicals and the early Victorians did not limit their goals to a mere self-defense against the flood of pornography. Inevitably, their drive to purify literature carried with it a deep suspicion of all imaginative writing. The book became the potential snare of the devil. When Thomas Bowdler took the blue pencil to Shakespeare, he was but reflecting the era's morbid concern with human passions.

Victorian censorship By the middle of the nineteenth century, Victorian censorship was in full swing. In the 1850s, book production became cheaper; and the reading public increased again. The expected happened: Editors began to press writers to treat sex in a gingerly fashion or, better still, not to treat it at all. Leslie Stephen, an editor, cautioned Thomas Hardy in the 1860s to "remember the country parson's daughters. *I* have always to remember them." In 1853, the English parliament passed the first act prohibiting the importation of pornography. The United States Congress had passed a similar statute in 1842. In 1857, Parliament passed the Campbell Act, which empowered magistrates to order the destruction of obscene books and prints. This was followed in the United States by the passing in 1865 of the first postal law prohibiting the distribution of obscene printed matter in the mails. In the same year a federal district court, acting under the 1842 customs law, prohibited the importation of shirt-front boxes embellished with a picture called "Susanna at the Bath" or "Diana and Her Nymphs." The govern-

[6]See Amy Cruse, *The Englishman and His Books in the Early Nineteenth Century*, George G. Harrap & Co. Ltd., London, 1930.

ment charged that the pictures were "too indelicate for family use."[7] All that remained to be done was to give a sweeping judicial definition to obscenity. The courts were quick to oblige.

The *Hicklin* test and "Comstockery" In 1868, Lord Cockburn handed down his famous decision in the *Hicklin* case. The new definition of obscenity was: "whether the tendency of the matter charged as obscene is to deprave and corrupt those whose minds are open to such immoral influences and into whose hands a publication of this sort may fall."[8] This meant that the starting point in the determination of obscenity was to be the moral level of a child. Furthermore, the court ruled that obscenity was not to be judged only by the tendency of the whole book, but also by isolated passages in the book.

In the United States, the *Hicklin* standard was quickly adopted; and, under the leadership of Anthony Comstock, a noble army of fanatics set out to rid American society of obscenity. To Comstock, obscenity was the great trap for the young, for "it breeds lust. Lust defiles the body, debauches the imagination, corrupts the mind; deadens the will, destroys the memory, sears the conscience, hardens the heart and damns the soul."[9] Like his evangelical forefathers, Comstock let his zeal carry him to excesses. The result was a general distrust of imaginative literature.

Under Comstock's leadership, the New York Society for the Suppression of Vice was founded in 1873. This was followed in 1874 by the founding of the Western Society for the Suppression of Vice; and in 1876, the New England Watch and Ward Society got under way in Boston. These societies, located in the principal publishing centers, were able to suppress books with the collaboration of the police. They became so powerful that they virtually dictated all the police arrests and even made citizens' arrests themselves. They suppressed everything from Whitman's *Leaves of Grass* and birth control literature to hard-core pornography. Comstock personally was able to boast that he had destroyed more than 50 tons of indecent books, 28,425 pounds of printing plates, and nearly 4 million obscene pictures!

It would be misleading to conclude from this that "Comstockery," a term introduced by G. B. Shaw, accounts for the romantic genteel tradition in American literature in the late nineteenth century. Comstockery was as much effect as it was cause. The genteel tradition was not the product of a single force but rather the product of movement and adjustment to the moral stresses of a rapidly industrialized society. Alice Rice's *Mrs. Wiggs of the Cabbage Patch* and Anthony's Hope's *The Prisoner of Zenda* were romantic escapades from the strains of the late Victorian era. Moreover, a great deal of Victorian censorship was cultural censorship privately imposed rather than public censorship. Indeed, with few exceptions the instincts of the literati were at one with those of the public in the 1860s and 1870s.

---

[7]*Anonymous*, No. 470, 1 Fed. Cas. 1024 (1865).
[8]*Queen v. Hicklin*, L.R. 3 O.B. 360, 371 (1868).
[9]Quoted Broun and Leach, in *Anthony Comstock*, p. 28.

The transition from reticence to realism in literature   As the Victorian period stretched on into the 1890s, a movement of protest against the genteel tradition arose. The family began to lose the place it had held under Victorianism; the drawing room and its reading habits were passing from existence; and a new generation of readers demanded the right to read what they liked—vice if they liked as well as virtue. Oscar Wilde said in his preface to *The Picture of Dorian Gray* in 1891: "Vice and virtue are to the artist material for his art. . . . There is no such thing as a moral or an immoral book. Books are well written or badly written." Authors on both sides of the Atlantic—Frank Norris, Theodore Dreiser, Thomas Hardy, G. B. Shaw, and James Joyce—broke away from the genteel tradition. They demanded the right to portray the bitterness and bleakness and not just the romance of their era. And this included a realistic or naturalistic approach to human passions.

The devotion of the new generation of authors to the rawness of human existence stirred the censors to new heights of activity. In retrospect, it is strange that the censors were so enraged by the new realism. The early realism in Anglo-American letters was not sex sensationalism. On the contrary, it frequently had a curious look of moral temperance and purity. True, sex was restored to the novel, but in the hands of a Frank Norris or a Thomas Hardy the new heroines were never sexual *and* moral.

It mattered little to the Comstocks's that many of the books they attacked in and out of the courts were indeed highly moralistic. What mattered to them was that human passions were being discussed for all the world, particularly the world of young ladies, to read about. Eventually, the censors went too far. Federal customs officials banned the importation of such classics as Balzac's *Droll Stories*, the complete works of Rabelais, Boccaccio's *Decameron*, Ovid's *Art of Love*, and Aristophanes' *Lysistrata*. The Post office even banned sex education materials, and the police attempted to ban Shaw's *Mrs. Warren's Profession*. Shaw concluded that the excess in censorship—Comstockery, as he called it—confirmed "the deep-seated conviction of the Old World that America is a provincial place, a second-rate country town civilization."[10] Comstock countered by calling Shaw an Irish smut peddler.

In part, Shaw's criticism missed the point by a country mile. The standards Shaw was criticizing were as English as John Bull. The important point was that mid-Victorian moral standards were on the way out—in the family, in the theater, and in the courts. The English *Hicklin* test, so widely adopted in the United States, was too restrictive for the twentieth century; and it was shortly to be attacked.

The first major judicial assault on the *Hicklin* rule was made in 1913 in an opinion by Judge Learned Hand. The case was a mail obscenity action brought in a federal district court against a book entitled *Hagar Revelly*. The novel is about the life of a young woman in New York who is compelled to earn her own living. She is represented as impulsive, sensuous, fond of pleasure, and restive under the monotony and squalor of her life. There is one unsuccessful and one successful seduction and

[10] Morris L. Ernest and William Seagle, *To the Pure*, Viking Press, New York, 1929. p. 60.

finally a loveless marriage. Judge Hand upheld the Post Office ban on the book simply because the *Hicklin* test had been accepted by the lower federal courts for more than thirty years, and he did not feel it proper at that date to disregard it. However, he did make this important observation:

> I hope it is not improper for me to say that the rule as laid down, however consonant it may be with mid-Victorian morals, does not seem to me to answer the understanding and morality of the present time, as conveyed by the words "obscene," "lewd," or "lascivious." I question whether in the end men will regard obscene that which is honestly relevant to the adequate expression of innocent ideas.[11]

In the year following Hand's decision, World War I began. This upheaval ended the already dying Victorian period. The full meaning of the change was not apparent for some time after the war, but the change could not be denied. American troops went to England and France, and the war was not all they were witness to. But before the pendulum could swing too far in the direction of a commonsense approach to obscenity cases, the censors had to expose to the public and the courts just how far they intended to go in controlling the reading matter of the mature public. In 1929, a general censorship wave hit Boston, and when it was over, sixty-eight books had been banned, including D. H. Lawrence's *Lady Chatterley's Lover*, Sherwood Anderson's *Dark Laughter*, Aldous Huxley's *Antic Hay*, Ernest Hemingway's *The Sun Also Rises*, and Theodore Dreiser's *An American Tragedy*. This was a grand finale to the 1920s.

From reticence to realism in the law   By the early 1930s, it was apparent that some modifications would have to be made in the law of obscenity. In 1930, Congress amended the Tariff Act to allow the Secretary of the Treasury to permit the admission of the classics or books of recognized literary merit, regardless of their alleged obscenity. Three years later a federal district court made the first successful attack on the *Hicklin* test.

In 1933, Judge John Woolsey in a United States district court in New York ruled that James Joyce's *Ulysses* was not obscene and lifted the ban on its importation. In lifting the ban, Judge Woolsey attacked the main thesis of the *Hicklin* test: the isolated-passages approach and the most-susceptible-person guide. He made the unprecedented move of reading the book himself. He found that there was a frankness in Joyce's approach, that portions of the book contained some dirty old Saxon words, and that the book as a whole did not have the leer of the sensualist. It was not "dirt for dirt's sake." On the contrary, he felt that the book was simply an honest attempt by means of a new literary method to describe the physical and mental life of the author's characters. While Judge Woolsey accepted a very broad definition of the word "obscene"—the tendency to stir sex impulses or to lead to sexually impure and lustful thoughts—he narrowed the application of the definition by

[11]*United States v. Kennedy*, 209 Fed. 119. 121 (1913).

conservative standards. First, he held that the court must consider the book as a whole and not isolated passages; and second, the book must be measured against its probable effect on a person with average sex instincts—against the normal person and not against the instincts of the perverted or the young.[12]

While the *Ulysses* case was an important breakthrough in the law of obscenity, it was only a lower federal court case, and as such it had to win adherents on the basis of its intrinsic soundness rather than on the basis of its precedence in the judicial hierarchy. The censorship picture in the United States is necessarily complicated by the nature of the federal system. There are two separate legal systems, state and federal. The federal government, as well as each state government, has its own obscenity laws. The picture is further complicated by the fact that, in addition to state statutes, many cities and counties have legislation governing obscenity. Thus there are literally hundreds of obscenity laws, each administered by separate law-enforcement agencies and interpreted by separate judicial systems. To the degree that uniformity is possible and desirable, it must come from the United States Supreme Court. After 1933, the *Ulysses* decision gained some recognition. However, the recognition was by no means uniform. For example, in 1954 Lillian Smith's *Strange Fruit* was banned in Massachusetts as obscene.[13] Three years later, in Pennsylvania, Erskine Caldwell's *God's Little Acre*, William Faulkner's *Sanctuary*, and James T. Farrell's *A World I Never Made* were cleared of obscenity charges.[14]

THE *ROTH* TEST

With the federal courts in conflict, some following the *Hicklin* rule and some following the *Ulysses* case, and with the state courts in an equal muddle, it was apparent that the United States Supreme Court would have to face the constitutional issue of censorship of obscenity. Before 1957, the Supreme Court had never squarely faced the issue of the censorship of obscene printed matter. In that year, the Court examined the validity of the federal mail statute that declares obscene printed matter to be nonmailable.[15] The Court upheld the validity of the statute and declared that obscenity is not within the area of constitutionally protected speech and press. The Court noted that historically the constitutional protection for freedom of the press was not considered to cover every utterance. It reasoned that "all ideas having the slightest redeeming social importance—unorthodox ideas, controversial ideas, even ideas hateful to the prevailing climate of opinion—have the full protection of the guarantees." But the Court concluded that obscenity is utterly without redeeming social importance.

The importance of the *Roth* case was not that it announced that obscenity is without constitutional protections; few people expected the Court to conclude otherwise. The importance of the case was in the

[12]*United States v. One Book Ulysses*, 5 F. Supp. 182 and 72 F.2d 705 (1934).
[13]*Commonwealth v. Isenstadt*, 318 Mass. 556 (1945).
[14]*Commonwealth v. Gordon*, 66 Pa. D. & C. 101 (1949).
[15]*Roth v. United States*, 354 U.S. 476 (1957).

attempt to establish a standard for measuring what is and what is not obscene. The Court rejected the *Hicklin* test. Instead, it cautioned that sex and obscenity are not synonymous. The protrayal of sex in art, literature, and scientific works is not itself sufficient reason to deny freedom of expression. On the other hand, "Obscene material is material which deals with sex in a manner appealing to prurient interest." In order that material that does not treat sex in such a manner may be protected, the Court established the following obscenity standard: whether to the average person, applying contemporary community standards, the dominant theme of the material taken as a whole appeals to prurient interest.

To the extent that the Court rejected the *Hicklin* test and substituted a more reasonable approach, the *Roth* case was certainly an improvement in the law of obscenity. However, the Court definition of obscenity in the *Roth* case left the law approximately where it was before—in a quandary. There is something circular in defining obscenity as that which appeals to prurient interest, for prurient is defined as lascivious, and lascivious as obscene. Perhaps the case is best viewed not as a definition of obscenity, but rather as an attitude that can serve as a guide. The spirit of the case is that while obscenity may be the valid subject of *postpublication* criminal sanctions, nonetheless the judiciary must carefully guard against illegal infringements on free speech and press. "Ceaseless vigilance is the watchword to prevent their erosion by Congress or by the States."

While the Court thus gave positive sanction to the right of a state to control obscenity, decisions after the *Roth* case often seemed contradictory and confusing.[16] This was particularly true after the so-called Fanny Hill Memoirs decision in 1966.[17] In the *Memoirs* decision a plurality of the Court attempted to graft on to the *Roth* rule a requirement that a prosecutor prove that a publication charged as obscene is *utterly* without redeeming social value.[18] As Justice White suggested in dissent, if social value is to be the test, then "Well written, especially effective obscenity is protected; the poorly written is vulnerable."[19]

THE HARD-CORE PORNOGRAPHY
TEST

By the end of the Warren Court era no one was particularly satisfied by the muddled state of the law of obscenity. On the one hand the Supreme Court had held that obscenity was not protected by the First Amendment. On the other hand the Court appeared to be moving in the direction of a legal standard that would, in effect, allow free circulation of everything except "hard-core pornography." The difficulty, as ever,

[16]See, *One, Inc. v. Olesen,* 355 U.S. 371 (1957). cf. *Mishkin v. New York,* 383 U.S, 502 (1966).
[17]*A Book Named John Cleland's Memoirs of a Woman of Pleasure v. Attorney General,* 383 U.S. 413.
[18]Ibid., p. 419
[19]Ibid., p. 461.

was in devising a satisfactory definition. Justice Stewart, an early proponent of the hard-core approach, observed that while he might never succeed in intelligently defining hard-core pornography, still, "I know it when I see it."[20]

The threshold problem did not dissuade a majority of the Burger Court from adopting this approach. In a series of decisions handed down in 1973 and 1974 the newly formed Burger majority adopted major revisions in the *Roth* test. Under the new *Miller* standard, hard-core pornography is defined in the following three-step process:

1 Whether the average person, applying contemporary community standards, would find that the work, taken as a whole, appeals to the prurient interest

2 Whether the work, taken as a whole, lacks serious literary, artistic, political, or scientific value

3 Whether the work depicts or describes, in a patently offensive way, sexual conduct specifically defined by the applicable state law[21]

Part 1 of the *Miller* test is simply a restatement of the *Roth* test. Part 2, however, rejects the amendment of the *Roth* test added by the *Fanny Hill* case. In the latter case, a plurality of the justices held that obscene material must be utterly without redeeming social value.[22] *Miller* rejected this element because it required the prosecution to prove a negative, that is, that the material in question was *utterly* without social value. The new Part 2 test not only reduces the prosecution's burden of proof, it also, as a practical matter, shifts part of the burden to the defense.

The shift in burden is made apparent by the opinions in two other cases decided by the Court on the same day as the *Miller* decision. In the *Paris* case a majority rejected the notion that the prosecution is required to produce "expert" affirmative evidence of the lack of serious literary or political value.[23] While the defense is free to introduce expert testimony, the prosecution need only introduce the materials alleged to be obscene.[24] Indeed, a footnote in the *Paris* case cast doubt on the use of expert testimony and quoted, approvingly, a lower court's observation that "Simply stated, hard-core pornography can and does speak for itself," an observation closely parallel to Justice Stewart's remark, "I know it when I see it."

Part 3 of the *Miller* test, the patently-offensive element, builds on a guideline first suggested by the late Justice Harlan in 1962.[25] Harlan's suggestion was later adopted by a plurality in the *Fanny Hill* case. The *Miller* test, however, offers specific guidelines for the determination of what is patently offensive sexual conduct. In *Miller* the Court suggested the following as *examples* of material that could meet this third element: "(a) patently offensive representations or descriptions of ultimate sexual acts, normal or perverted, actual or simulated or (b) patently

[20]Concurring in *Jacobellis v. Ohio*, 378 U.S. 184, 197 (1964).

[21]*Miller v. California*, 93 S.Ct. 2607 (1973).

[22]*Memoirs v. Massachusetts*, 383 U.S. 413, 418 (1966).

[23]*Paris Adult Theatre v. Slaton*, 93 S.Ct. 2628 (1973).

[24]*Kaplan v. California*, 93 S.Ct. 2680, 2685 (1973).

[25]See *Manual Enterprises v. Day*.

offensive representations or descriptions of masturbation, excretory functions, and lewd exhibition of the genitals.[26]

These examples would appear to be the gravamen of the *Miller* test. Indeed, the opinion went on to state that "no one will be subject to prosecution for the sale or exposure of obscene materials unless these materials depict or describe patently offensive "hard-core" sexual conduct."[27] The point was reiterated by the Court in the following year when the Georgia ban on the film *Carnal Knowledge* was overturned. Justice Rehnquist, speaking for a unanimous Court, said the *Miller* examples of patently offensive, while not an exhaustive catalog, were, nonetheless, "intended to fix substantive constitutional limitations deriving from the First Amendment."[28]

Finally, the *Miller* case rejected a *national* community standard as a constitutional requirement. Chief Justice Burger observed that:

> It is neither realistic nor constitutionally sound to read the First Amendment as requiring that the people of Maine or Mississippi accept public depiction of conduct found tolerable in Las Vegas or New York City. . . . People in different states vary in their tastes and attitudes, and this diversity is not to be strangled by the absolutism of imposed uniformity.[29]

While the *Miller* case rejected a uniform national community standard as unrealisitc, the majority opinion was unclear as to the geographic parameters of "community." A statewide community standard was permitted in the *Miller* case. One year later the Court said that no precise geographic area is required as a matter of constitutional law. Rather, the juror in applying the standard of the "average person in the contemporary community" may "draw on knowledge of the community or vicinage from which he comes."[30] In other words, the Court acknowledges that under what is presumably a local community standard, publishers and distributors may be subjected to varying community standards in the different judicial districts into which they transmit materials, always assuming, however, that the jury does not "have unbridled discretion in determining what is 'patently offensive.'"[31] Furthermore, a post-*Miller* decision has also indicated that the average-person test is not open-ended. While a judge may instruct a jury that the contemporary community includes the sensitive and the insensitive, the instruction may not *focus* on the most susceptible or sensitive member of the community.[32] To allow such a focus would, of course, be a return to the nineteenth-century *Hicklin* standard. The Court has also ruled that the average person means the average adult, and therefore a jury is precluded from considering children as a part of the relevant community, at least where

---

[26]*Miller v. California*, 93 S.Ct. 2615 (1973).
[27]Ibid., p. 2616.
[28]*Jenkins v. Georgia*, 94 S.Ct. 2750, 2755 (1974).
[29]*Miller v. California*, 93 S.Ct. 2619–2620 (1973).
[30]*Hamling v. United States*, 94 S.Ct. 2887, 2901 (1974).
[31]*Jenkins v. Georgia*, 94 S.Ct. 2755 (1974).
[32]*Pinkus v. United States*, 98 S.Ct. 1808 (1978).

it is evident that children are not the intended recipients of the materials in litigation.[33]

FREEDOM OF EXPRESSION AND THE *MILLER* TEST

The *Miller* test attempts to bring clarity to areas that had been hopelessly confused. The mere fact that a majority of the justices finally agreed on a new test was something of a victory for craftmanship and it may well reduce some of the uncertainty that plagued obscenity cases throughout the 1960s. Yet the formula still attempts to describe the forbidden by concepts that are so elusive that they are uniquely unsuited to the criminal law. As Justice Brennan noted in his *Miller* dissent, the vagueness inherent in the phrases "prurient interest," "patently offensive," "lewd exhibition," "pandering," "community standard," and "serious literary value" suggest that the test is far from the kind of sensitive tool necessary under the First Amendment to separate the protected from the unprotected.

The vagueness of the *Miller* formula can produce two undesirable results. First, since it fails to provide adequate notice to publishers, distributors, and sellers, it thus compels them to guess whether their conduct is covered by the criminal law. When conduct is made criminal, the law should be sufficiently definite so that a person of ordinary intelligence will have fair notice that his conduct is forbidden. It is doubtful whether "prurient interest," "patently offensive," and "serious literary value" reduce the uncertainty to a level consonant with freedom of expression. Secondly, the vagueness creates a likelihood that the uncertainty of the law will have a spill-over effect on materials that are protected. As a practical matter the formula leaves a wide area of law-enforcement discretion to the police and prosecutor, so wide that it is highly probable that in the normal course of enforcement, protected materials will be at least temporarily banned. Furthermore, to create this type of uncertainty in a criminal statute may well lead publishers and distributors to overcompensate for the vagueness by engaging in self-censorship. The potential chilling effect of a *Miller*-type formula creates a serious threat to freedom of expression. The vice of vagueness in a criminal statute is compounded when the statute applies to the area of expression.

Still, the *Miller* case represents a serious attempt by a majority of the justices of the Supreme Court to clarify the law of obscenity. The attempt to circumscribe the area of permissable regulation and to provide a set of guidelines for prosecutors and juries is laudable. However, the rationale of *Miller* and related cases reveals the fundamental weakness of attempts by the state to regulate obscene publications. Briefly stated, the rationale of the new hard-core pornography test, as stated by Chief Justice Burger, is that

> there are legitimate state interests at stake in stemming the tide of commercialized obscenity. . . . These include the interest of the public in the quality

of life and the total community environment, the tone of commerce in the great city centers, and, possibly, the public safety itself. The Hill-Link Minority Report of the Commission on Obscenity and Pornography indicates that there is at least an arguable correlation between obscene material and crime. . . . Although there is no conclusive proof of a connection between antisocial behavior and obscene material, the legislature . . . could quite reasonably determine that such a connection does or might exist. . . . From the beginning of civilized societies, legislators and judges have acted on various unprovable assumptions. . . . The fact that a [legislative] directive reflects unprovable assumptions about what is good for the people, including imponderable aesthetic assumptions, is not a sufficient reason to find that statute unconstitutional. . . . The sum of experience, including that of the last two decades, affords an ample basis for legislatures to conclude that a sensitive, key relationship of human experience, central to family life, community welfare, and the development of human personality, can be debased and distorted by crass commercial exploitation of sex. Nothing in the Constitution prohibits a state from reaching such a conclusion and acting on it legislatively simply because there is no conclusive evidence or empirical data.[34]

The rationale is twofold. First, there is the argument that even in the absence of conclusive evidence, legislatures are constitutionally free to infer a causal relationship between obscenity and antisocial behavior. While this was the major legislative argument for many years, it was not endorsed by a majority of the Supreme Court until 1973. The irony of the argument is that the Court would endorse it just at a time when empirical evidence was beginning to suggest the opposite conclusion. Indeed, in this regard, the majority opinion's reliance on the Hill-Link minority report was quite misplaced. True, the Hill-Link report refused to accept the conclusion that exposure to explicit sexual materials played no significant role in the causation of delinquent or criminal behavior. Still Commissioners Hill and Link stated, "We believe it is impossible and totally unnecessary, to attempt to prove or disprove a cause-effect relationship between pornography and criminal behavior. We believe that pornography has an eroding effect on society, on public morality, on respect for human worth, on attitudes toward family love, on culture."[35] In the final analysis, then, the Supreme Court justices' argument is essentially the same as the argument made by the Hill-Link report, that is, one of moral denunciation of the indecency of pornography. Simply put, this argument holds that pornography is moral pollution, a pollution that reduces love to sex and persons to mere objects: a pollution that destroys privacy, sensitivity, and nobility and replaces these with a shameless and gross voyeurism, and all to make a profit. The argument is both moral and aesthetic. It is an argument that suggests that civility in our society depends on the maintenance of a certain standard of common decency, a decency without which the family cannot survive; a decency which allows art to triumph over trash. Doubtless

[34]*Paris Adult Theatre v. Slaton*, 93 S.Ct. 2635, 2638 (1973).
[35]*Report of the President's Commission on Obscenity and Pornography*, 1970, p. 306.

civility, privacy, love, and human dignity are values that are to be cherished over lust and lewdness. Yet, where is the evidence that America has been a more decent, civil, and noble society because of obscenity legislation? Furthermore, the argument fails to confront the profoundly troubling mechanical problems of translating these good intentions into concrete results, particularly when the translation is to be accomplished by the use of criminal law.

Assuming, for purposes of argument, that the *Miller* test is a sensitive instrument for separating the unprotected from the protected—that the definitions of hard-core are precise and limited—and that the test will be used by state and federal agencies only in the elimination of patently offensive hard-core pornography, we are still confronted with the issue of whether the government should, consistent with the First Amendment, censor such materials. At the outset we are faced with the specter of the government screening materials to determine whether they have "serious literary or political value." From a practical point of view the screening is done by police and district attorneys. Even assuming a deep commitment on their part to the First Amendment and a keen sensitivity to aesthetic and polictical issues, it is difficult to justify conferring such unbound screening power upon law-enforcement officers. Nor does the fact that judges or juries will make the ultimate decisions resolve the problem. Presumably, in a free society, literary and political values are coins traded in a free market and not in police stations and jury rooms.

Finally, the *Miller* test, like the earlier *Roth* test, asks us to make a great leap of faith. We are to believe that the elimination of hard-core pornography will produce a more decent and civil society. Unless, however, we have some reasonably conclusive evidence of the harmful consequences of pornography, some First Amendment consideration should be given to those who wish to read and view such materials. There is some evidence to suggest that the size of this audience is not insignificant. Pornography may be their private damnation, but an important premise of the First Amendment is that free citizens normally make their own choices. So long as freedom of choice here does not invade the privacy of unconsenting adults or impose itself on children, it should be allowed to operate in the marketplace. The justification of pruriency, of lewdness, or morbidity and shame is the thinly disguised appeal of a tyranny by those who would, through the criminal law, uplift our spirits and improve our minds. Yet the First Amendment took that proscriptive and prescriptive power out of the hands of the government. Freedom of expression protects trash, and it does so by wisely protecting the power of adult citizens to make up their own categories of "trash" and "nontrash."

CONCLUSION

It is easy to become disturbed about the tasteless and indeed decadent quality of the material offered by some of our newsstands and theaters. It is equally easy to worry about the erosion of traditional moral standards. However, as we approach the end of the twentieth century, one thing should become apparent: Governments committed to freedom of expression are ill-equipped to preserve artistic taste or conventional standards of private morality. The fact of the matter is that governmental suppression of plays, films, books, and magazines simply does not work. Suppression creates at least as many problems as it attempts to solve. In the process, suppression gives the "sexploitation" magazines, books, and films the quality of forbidden fruit and thereby helps to sustain a market for materials that otherwise merit oblivion. The vast market for these materials is a further indication of the weakness of suppression. We should not make criminal, or outlaw, matters in which there is no substantial social consensus, particularly when we are uncertain about the antisocial impact of the matter. From the basis of our own private religious or ethical positions, we may regret "lustful" or "impure" thoughts, yet in a free society we should pause to consider whether one person's lustful thought might not be another person's evening of pleasant reading. However useful the terms "obscenity," "pornography," "lewdness," and "lustfulness" may be in conventional language, they belong in a private world from which a democratic government should be excluded.

> A popular Government, without popular information or the means of acquiring it, is but a prologue to a farce or a tragedy; or perhaps both.
>
> —*James Madison*

THE PRESS AND ACCESS TO INFORMATION

It is generally conceded that freedom of the press is not an absolute; that is, it does not carry with it the right to operate beyond or outside of the law. Even the most central part of the freedom, the freedom to publish, is not an absolute. As we have noted above, obscenity laws act as constraints, normally in the form of postpublication civil or criminal penalties. Libel law is yet another form of restraint.[36] Beyond these constraints, however, there is the issue of whether the press is constitutionally entitled to access to information, an entitlement beyond what the normal individual enjoys. In some sense the press discharges a societal function that transcends the individual. In consequence, does this public interest function entitle the press to greater access to information, especially information controlled by the government? This is a particularly crucial issue in a society where the executive branch of the government is at once large and not always immediately accountable for its actions. If the public is entitled to know what the government is doing, it cannot always depend on the government to come forward with all of the information that is necessary in order to make judgments. To this end, we often turn to the press. One only has to look at recent chapters in American history, namely Watergate and Vietnam, to realize the importance of the press to the goal of public accountability of the government.

On the other hand, few would dispute that the government often must, in the public interest, close its doors to the press. Secrecy, privacy, and

---

[36] See *New York Times v. Sullivan*, 376 U.S. 254 (1964).

confidentiality in government are neither novel nor necessarily inconsistent with a free press. Of course, restricted access will reduce the fund of available information, but, as Chief Justice Warren once noted, "There are few restrictions on action which could not be clothed by ingenious argument in the garb of decreased data flow. . . . The right to speak and publish does not carry with it the unrestrained right to gather information."[37] The press can still serve its societal function and yet not be allowed access, for example, to the proceedings of a grand jury or the Joint Chiefs of Staff or the deliberations of the justices of the United States Supreme Court.

To pose the question in absolute terms of either no access by the press greater than a private individual's or unrestrained access by the press is to ignore the complexity of the issue. Unfortunately the Court has chosen to examine the issue in absolute terms. In *Pell v. Procunier*, the Court confronted a California prison regulation that placed an absolute ban on media access to specific individual prison inmates.[38] The press had wanted to interview specific prisoners on a mutually agreeable basis, whereas the prison regulation allowed media acces only to prisoners randomly selected by prison officials. The majority was obviously impressed by the state's argument that penal interest required such a regulation. It was the state's contention that media attention on specific prisoners can cause disciplinary problems, particularly when the attention exalts certain prisoners as public figures, thereby increasing their influence within the prison population. Such an argument is not without merit, particularly in view of the access to prisoners that California prison regulations otherwise allow. Had the *Pell* majority simply chosen to accept the ban as a reasonable restriction on the manner of prisoner accessibility to the media, it would have been an unexceptionable decision. Instead, the *Pell* majority chose to write large and ruled that:

> The Constitution does not . . . require government to accord the press special access to information not shared by members of the public generally. It is one thing to say that a journalist is free to seek out sources of information not available to members of the general public, that he is entitled to some constitutional protection of the confidentiality of such sources . . . and that government cannot restrain the publication of news emanating from such sources. It is quite another thing to suggest that the Constitution imposes upon government the affirmative duty to make available to journalists sources of information not available to members of the public generally. That proposition finds no support in the words of the Constitution or in any decision of this Court.[39]

The *Pell* decision appears to cast the issue in terms of either an uninhibited press license to interview at will all prisoners or an absolute ban in order to promote prison discipline. What the majority failed to

---

[37]*Zemel v. Rusk*, 381 U.S. 1, 16–17 (1965); see also Note, "The Right of the Public and the Press to Gather Information," *Harvard Law Review*, vol. 87, p. 1505, 1974.
[38]*Pell v. Procunier*, 417 U.S. 817 (1974).
[39]Ibid., p. 834.

consider was whether the ban in *Pell* was consonant with the societal role of a free press. An absolute ban precludes accurate and effective reporting of prison conditions—a question of some public importance. It is also a self-serving regulation to the extent that it makes the administrative lives of prison officials less subject to the glare of media exposure. Surely penal interests and the interests of the press can be served by regulations less restrictive than an absolute ban on media access to named prisoners.[40]

The issue reappeared in 1978, this time in the form of a request by a television station to investigate conditions in a county jail, the site of a recent prisoner suicide. While there was only a plurality opinion in *Houchins v. KQED*, the opinion of Chief Justice Burger was as unrelenting as the *Pell* opinion. Burger again asserted that:

> The public importance of conditions in penal facilities and the media's role of providing information afford no basis for reading into the Constitution a right of the public or the media to enter these institutions, with camera equipment, and take moving and still pictures of inmates for broadcast purposes. This Court has never intimated a First Amendment guarantee of a right of access to all sources of information within government control.[41]

It is certainly true, as Chief Justice Burger argued, that media access to prisons is an appropriate question for the legislative and executive branches of the government. But that could be said equally of access to parks, streets, and other public facilities. The question rather is whether prison access regulations made by either the executive or the legislative branch must give some constitutional deference to a limited right of the press to gather information about the operation of a public institution. It may be that the high purposes of government are often served by secrecy, but then, so too are purposes not so noble.

PROTECTING CONFIDENTIAL SOURCES AND THE EDITORIAL PROCESS

Secrecy is a two-way street. The press, in serving a societal role, often thinks it necessary to intrude into areas from which it is normally excluded. On the other hand, the press sometimes resists intrusion by the government into its operations. Indeed, the press in the United States has not been unwilling to draw a rather large circle around its operations, claiming a zone of exemption from the rules that might otherwise apply. At various times press associations or newspapers have attempted, without success, to use freedom of the press as a basis for immunity from antitrust legislation, collective bargaining laws, and minimum wage legislation.[42] Yet, all that the First Amendment clause does is to ensure

[40]See also *Saxbe v. The Washington Post*, 417 U.S. 843 (1974).
[41]*Houchins v. KQED*, 98 S.Ct. 2588, 2594 (1978).
[42]*Associated Press v. United States*, 326 U.S. 1 (1945), application of the Sherman Anti-Trust Act; *Associated Press v. NLRB*, 301 U.S. 103 (1937), application of the National Labor Relations Act of 1935; *Oklahoma Press v. Walling*, 327 U.S. 186 (1946), application of the Fair Labor Standards Act.

that the government will not use its rule-making and rule-enforcing powers to control or destroy the press, either by sophisticated or simple-minded devices. Thus, the press is subject to the ordinary application of the laws so long as it is apparent that the law is not attempting to silence or control the press. For example, may a business license tax be, applied in such a way as to act as a prior restraint on the press? In *Grosjean v. American Press*, Louisiana imposed a 2 percent gross receipts tax on newspapers with a daily circulation of over 20,000.[43] In striking down this legislation, which the Court equated to "tax on Knowledge," the Court was careful not to rule that newspapers are exempt from ordinary forms of taxation. The key to the *Grosjean* ruling was not the 2 percent gross receipts tax but the triggering device of newspapers with over 20,000 in circulation. In simple terms, it was a deliberate attempt to silence the political opposition to Senator Huey Long. The Long forces were dominant in the small towns and rural areas but not in New Orleans, the only city with newspapers with circulations in excess of 20,000. While the opinion did not directly mention the internal political struggle of Louisiana, it did do so obliquely by noting that the plain purpose of the tax was to penalize and curtail the circulation of a selected group of publishers.

While the *Grosjean* case is often cited for its defense of a free press, neither the *Grosjean* decision nor any subsequent decision has suggested that the press enjoys any special exemptions from the ordinary application of laws and rules. That, of course, was the position adopted in the prison access cases, and it was also the position adopted in the controversy over protecting a reporter's confidential sources of information.

In *Branzburg v. Hayes*, a Louisville, Kentucky, reporter published a story about two unnamed local residents who were active in the business of synthesizing hashish from marijuana.[45] Shortly thereafter, Branzburg was subpoenaed to appear before the county grand jury. When the grand jury requested that he identify the individuals in his story, he refused. Some weeks later Branzburg wrote another story about drug users in Kentucky, and he was again summoned before a grand jury. This time he refused to appear on the grounds that to disclose confidences gathered in his investigation of the drug culture would destroy a relationship of trust, and he would thereby be vitally hampered in any subsequent attempt to report in that area. In short, Branzburg was asking the judiciary to carve out a testimonial privilege for reporters to protect confidential information obtained in trust, a privilege not unlike that enjoyed by doctors, lawyers, and members of the clergy. A bare majority of the Court refused to graft such a privilege on to the First Amendment. Justice White, writing for the majority, concluded:

> On the records now before us, we perceive no basis for holding that the public interest in law enforcement and in ensuring effective grand jury proceedings is insufficient to override the consequential, but uncertain, burden

[43]*Grosjean v. American Press*, 297 U.S. 233 (1936).
[44]Ibid., p. 251.
[45]*Branzburg v. Hayes*, 408 U.S. 665 (1972); there were two companion cases decided with *Branzburg*, *In re Poppas* and *United States v. Caldwell*.

on news gathering that is said to result from insisting that reporters, like other citizens, respond to relevant questions put to them in the course of a valid grand jury investigation or criminal. . . . Grand juries address themselves to the issues of whether crimes have been committed and who committed them. Only where news sources themselves are implicated in crime or possess information relevant to the grand jury's task need they or the reporter be concerned about grand jury subpoenas. . . . The preference for anonymity of those confidential informants involved in actual criminal conduct is presumably a product of their desire to escape criminal prosecution, and this preference, while understandable, is hardly deserving of constitutional protection. It would be frivolous to assert—and no one does in these cases—that the First Amendment, in the interest of securing news or otherwise, confers a license on either the reporter or his news sources to violate valid criminal laws. . . . Thus, we cannot seriously entertain the notion that the First Amendment protects a newsman's agreement to conceal the criminal conduct of his source, or evidence thereof, on the theory that it is better to write about crime than to do something about it.[46]

Surely, Justice Stewart, writing in dissent, was right when he argued that a corollary of the right to publish is the right to gather information. It is debatable, however, whether a reporter's privilege is a corollary of the right to gather information. The right to gather information, even confidential information, is not one uniquely enjoyed by reporters. If there is a privilege to refuse to divulge confidential information, it arises out of the right to gather information, and thus it would seem logical to extend that privilege to all who enjoy that right. In any event, it would be safe to predict that if a reporter's constitutional privilege is accepted, others will demand an equal privilege derivative of the same information-gathering right. Perhaps a more appropriate solution to the problem of protecting confidential sources of information is to provide a statutory authorized privilege, a so-called reporter's shield law. Constitutional testimonial privileges often have to be stated in absolute terms, and modification is an awkward and slow process.

On the other hand, a legislative solution could respond to such a problem as who is a reporter. Defining who qualifies for such a privilege, particularly in a profession that is almost necessarily unlicensed, would appear to be the sort of problem best left to the discretion of legislatures. (At the time of *Branzburg*, seventeen states had such statutes.)

If a reporter has no unique right to withhold information from a grand jury, then it would seem plausible that other individuals in the media process would be subject to an equal rule. The problem was confronted in a 1979 case, *Herbert v. Lando*.[47] In 1969–70, Anthony Herbert, a retired Army officer, received widespread media attention when he accused his superiors of war crimes in Vietnam. Some years later CBS broadcast a report on Herbert that could have been construed as por-

---

[46]Ibid., pp. 690–692; subsequently the Court has refused opportunities to limit the *Branzburg* decision, e.g., *New York Times v. Jascalevich*, 99 S.Ct. 6 (1978), Justices Marshall and White as circuit justices.

[47]*Herbert v. Lando*, 99 S.Ct. 1635.

traying him as a liar. The report was produced and edited by Barry Lando. Herbert sued Lando, CBS, and others for defamation. Since Herbert was not an ordinary private citizen, but rather, for purposes of libel law, a public figure, he could receive an award only if he could prove "actual malice," in the publication of a damaging falsehood.[48] Proving actual malice presents a difficult evidentiary problem for a plaintiff. How could Herbert prove it unless he could discover whether Lando had any reason to doubt the veracity of any of his sources or if Lando had made any selection based on a preference for the veracity of one source rather than others? In other words, how could Herbert prove that Lando had acted in malice unless Herbert could go back into the editorial process and discover Lando's state of mind as he edited the program. Under libel law, Lando would not be liable to a judgment unless Herbert could prove that he must have known or had reason to suspect that he was publishing false material about Herbert.

If we are to have libel laws, it would seem that there must be some appropriate process that would allow Herbert to discover whether in the editorial process, Lando had entertained doubts about the accuracy of the material. If Herbert's reputation had been defamed with actual malice, then he needed a public forum for vindiction. On the other hand, to intrude into the editorial process, especially regarding material that was *not* published, could have a chilling effect on the future course of broadcast and print journalism. If journalists and editors know that their prepublication conservations are subject to discovery in defamation suits, they may engage in self-censorship to such a degree that the final publication product is timid. Yet even Justice Marshall noted in his dissent in the *Herbert* case:

> At best, it can be argued only that failure to insulate the press from this form of disclosure will inhibit not the editing process but the final product—that. the specter of questions concerning opinion and belief will induce journalists to refrain from publishing material thought to be accurate. . . . So long as *Sullivan* makes state of mind dispositive, some inquiry as to the manner in which decisions are made is inevitable. And it is simply implausible to suppose that asking a reporter why certain material was or was not included in a given publication will be more likely to stifle incisive journalism than compelling disclosure of other objective evidence regarding that decision.[49]

In upholding Herbert's right to discover prepublication editorial conversations, the Court predicated its decision on the continuing need in our society for the protection of an individual's reputation. To erect an impenetrable barrier in the way of an "editorial privilege" would substantially reduce a plaintiff's ability to prove culpability on the part of the defendant. The majority noted, however, that its decision should not be construed as supporting casual inquiry into the editorial process, noting that "There is no law that subjects the editorial process to pri-

---

[48]The actual malice rule in libel cases was announced in *New York Times v. Sullivan*, 376 U.S. 254 (1964), and the public figure rule in *Curtis Publishing v. Butts*, 388 U.S. 130 (1967).
[49]*Herbert v. Lando*, 99 S.Ct. 1665.

vate or official examination merely to satisfy curiosity or to serve some general end such as the public interest."[50]

Whether the *Herbert* decision will prove to have a serious chilling effect on the media remains to be seen. Clearly one chilling effect that the Court intended its decision to have is an inhibition on the publishing of knowing or reckless falsehoods that damage individual reputations.

To some the *Branzburg* and *Herbert* decisions may give the appearance of judicial insensitiveness to the needs of the press. In fairness to the Burger Court it should, however, be noted that the Court has handed down a number of other opinions that have been strongly supportive of a free press. Thus, in *New York Times v. United States*, the Court struck down the injunction the federal government had obtained to prevent further publication of the so-called Pentagon Papers,[51] and in 1976 the Court struck down a trial court's "gag press" order that would have restrained the press from publishing information about a pending criminal trial.[52] The Court has also supported the media against claims of a right of access to the press. Thus, in *C.B.S. v. Democratic National Committee*, the Court ruled that broadcasters could not be forced to accept editorial advertisements, and in 1974 it struck down a Florida law that forced a newspaper to give a free right of reply to any political candidate whose personal character or official record had been attacked by the newspaper.[53] Finally, in 1980 the Court retreated from an earlier decision and held that in the absence of an overriding interest articulated in the findings, neither the press nor public may be excluded from a criminal trial. Relying on Anglo-American traditions of publicity and open trials, Chief Justice Burger wrote, " . . . in the context of trials . . . the First Amendment guarantees of speech and press, standing alone, prohibit government from summarily closing courtroom doors. . . ."[54]

A free pass is still vital to free society, but the claims made by the press are not to be taken as substitutes for an argument. There are other values and societal needs that must be considered when claims of a free press are pushed, especially when the claim is pushed by associations and enterprises with vast accumulations of unreviewable power. A free press has legitimate needs in gathering and publishing information, and it would be constitutionally short-sighted not to recognize the requirements of a free press. We should also recognize, however, that the enterprises of the press will rather naturally attempt to draw a wide circle around their operations and to label that circle a zone in which the press is free of any competing claims, private or public.

---

[50]Ibid., p. 1648.

[51]*New York Times v. United States,* 403 U.S. 713 (1971).

[52]*Nebraska Press Association v. Stuart,* 427 U.S. 539 (1976); see also *Cox Broadcasting v. Cohn,* 420 U.S. 469 (1975).

[53]*Columbia Broadcasting System v. Democratic National Committee,* 412 U.S. 94 (1973); *Miami Herald v. Tornillo,* 418 U.S. 241.

[54]*Richmond Newspapers Inc. v. Virginia,* 48 U.S. Law Week 5008, 5013 (1980); cf. *Gannett v. DePasquale,* 99 S.Ct. 2898 (1979).

3 FREEDOM OF EXPRESSION

There is nothing like stridency, anger, irresponsible behavior, and some questionable moral platitudes to make one question the democratic faith in freedom of expression. Yet we have been committed to this faith for nearly two hundred years, ever since we declared that men have "certain unalienable Rights, that among these are Life, Liberty, and the pursuit of Happiness." But faith it is. We believe in freedom of expression but we cannot empirically test the accuracy of the underlying premises. We accept on faith that freedom of expression is necessary as a means to individual self-fulfillment. A contemporary democratic theorist, Sir Ernest Barker, stated the premise thusly: "The essence of liberty will be that it is a condition, or status, or quality, which individual personality must possess in order that it may translate itself from what it is to what it has the capacity of becoming."[1]

Additionally, we believe in freedom of expression because we assume that it is essential in the search for knowledge and the discovery of truth. Justice Oliver Wendell Holmes stated that "the ultimate good is reached by free trade in ideas—that the best test of truth is the power of the thought to get itself accepted in the competition of the market."[2] Furthermore, we assume that only through the framework of the free and open discussion of public policy can a democratic society avert those kinds of cleavages that suppress dissent, fail to make adequate responses to genuine problems, and that ultimately will destroy the society.

Finally, the principle of freedom of expression is a natural corollary of our program of self-government. In a free state, public issues and public policies are to be openly debated and decided by the people and their representatives.

The above, then, constitute some of the basic assumptions of freedom of expression. As a nation, our practices have not infrequently strayed from the logical paths of these assumptions, but we have never disavowed our basic faith in the principle of freedom of expression.

Our faith in the value of freedom of expression led us to adopt the First Amendment: "Congress shall make no law respecting an establishment of religion, or prohibiting the free exercise thereof; or abridging the freedom of speech, or of the press; or of the right of the people peaceably to

[1]Ernest Barker, *Reflections on Government*, Oxford University Press, London, 1942, p. 16.
[2]Dissenting in *Abrams v. United States*, 250 U.S. 616 (1919).

assemble, and to petition the government for a redress of grievances."[3] The various rights noted in the First Amendment collectively constitute the right to freedom of expression.

A THEORY OF FREEDOM OF EXPRESSION

The practice of freedom is local, while the theory of freedom should be national.[4] That is, as citizens we generally exercise our rights in political broadsides distributed on local streets and in speeches in our hometown parks and public meeting places. Few of us can command the resources of the national communications media. The sprightly Fourth of July parade or the sometimes strident antiwar speech compete locally with a host of other important social interests. The security of streets, the privacy of the home, the right to shop and move about freely in business districts, the sanctuary of a quiet corner in a public park, all these are subject to stresses resulting from freedom of expression. The tests of freedom and the first and generally the final decisions about freedom of expression are made locally.

Given the diversity of American communities, there should be some national theoretical framework to which private citizens, local judges, and other public officers could turn to for guidance in coping with the many novel and complex issues of freedom of expression. We are one nation, and the Constitution should provide the necessary first step in developing such a theoretical framework. Development of the theory should be the responsibility of the United States Supreme Court. However, as Prof. Thomas Emerson has observed, the Court has failed to develop any comprehensive, coherent theory of the First Amendment. The Court, particularly during the years that Earl Warren was Chief Justice, made numerous declarations favoring freedom of expression, such as those decisions curbing legislative investigating committees,[5] limiting state loyalty oaths,[6] rendering ineffective provisions of the Internal Security Act,[7] and ensuring that the First Amendment keep pace with changing economic and cultural developments.[8]

Still, the task of constructing a theoretical framework for freedom of expression is important. Lip service to the value of freedom of expression will not help to resolve the myriad controversies that arise when we attempt to adapt this value to a host of other local and national interests. Without a proper framework, the right to freedom of expression frequently amounts to nothing more than the right to cheer the majority on. The

---

[3]The requirements of the First Amendment apply equally to the states through the due process clause of the Fourteenth Amendment [*Gitlow v. New York* 268 U.S. 652 (1925), and subsequent cases].

[4]"Theory" here is not used in the sense of a set of hypotheses but rather as a standard or test.

[5]*Watkins v. United States*, 354 U.S. 178 (1957).

[6]*Elfbrandt v. Russell*, 384 U.S. 11 (1966).

[7]For example, *Albertson v. Subversive Activities Control Board*, 382 U.S. 70 (1965).

[8]*Amalgamated Food Employees v. Logan Valley Plaza*, 391 U.S. 308 (1968); *Tinker v. Des Moines Independent School District*, 393 U.S. 503 (1969).

status quo, as represented by mayors, chiefs of police, city managers, park directors, judges, school boards, city councils, and state legislatures will, quite naturally, and not always without good reasons, resist change. The status quo has the power, authority, and legitimacy of the law; and it has a distinct tendency to use the resources of the law to protect other social interests first, giving them priority over the right to dissent.

Society cannot operate without a degree of unity and consensus. There must be a fair degree of stability in society. The rules, the laws, and administrative regulations cannot change on a daily basis; if they did, citizens could not anticipate the consequences of their actions. The stable society affords us the opportunity to plan our lives with some degree of certainty. But the genuine need for unity and stability should not become a cloak for a fossilized political structure and a legal system that amounts to congealed injustice. Faced with the reality of social forces pushing limits on the right to freedom of expression, we need a coherent legal theory of the First Amendment as a starting point from which we can begin any particular discussion of limiting the right. The legal system then can act, not simply as a means of social control of individual or group behavior, but equally as a control on the behavior of the government.

Expression and action   At the outset it must be recognized that a system of free expression necessarily involves public controversy. Indeed, the First Amendment serves one of its highest functions when it fosters conflict and channels it into peaceful methods of persuasion. As Justice William O. Douglas has stated:

> A function of free speech under our system of government is to invite dispute. It may indeed best serve its high purpose when it induces a condition of unrest, creates dissatisfaction with conditions as they are, or even stirs people to anger. Speech is often provocative and challenging. It may strike at prejudices and preconceptions and have profound unsettling effects as it presses for acceptance of an idea.[9]

If a system of freedom of expression is to have any reality, we must accept that it protects those who espouse unpopular, radical, and unconventional ideas. And further, we must expect that those who espouse such ideas will frequently resort to bitter and hostile language, language likely to arouse other members of the community. The language of the status quo generally appeals to our more rational side, whereas the language of unconventional causes is more likely to appeal to our emotions. We cannot expect black militants or Chicanos to press their views in the language of the drawing room. The politics of conventional causes rarely approaches the boderline of disorder; the politics of radical causes rarely leaves this borderline. If we are to have a true "free marketplace of ideas," then we must accept the unsettling effects, the temporary disruptions of "business as usual," this borderline of disorder that is central to the preservation of open channels of communication.

[9]*Terminiello v. Chicago*, 337 U.S. 1 (1949).

Yet a system of freedom of expression protects expression and not action. The government may, within limits of due process, limit our actions but not our expressions. Society need not and cannot tolerate disorder. The dividing line between "expression" and "action" is not always easy to draw. Both are forms of conduct. But as Thomas Emerson has persuasively suggested, it is closer to the spirit of the First Amendment than the ad hoc tests of "clear and present danger," "incitement," and "balancing" on which the Supreme Court has tended to rely.[10]

Occasionally, the Supreme Court has attempted to distinguish "pure speech" from "conduct." In a case construing the Smith Act, the Court held that the advocacy of the "abstract doctrine" of the violent overthrow of government was constitutionally protected, whereas the advocacy of action toward that end was subject to governmental regulation. The Court observed: "The essential distinction is that those to whom the advocacy is addressed must be urged to *do* something, now or in the future, rather than to believe in something."[11]

This distinction between "pure speech" and "conduct" goes back to certain Court decisions involving picketing in labor-management disputes.[12] In recent years the Court has seized upon these earlier decisions and applied them to a series of civil rights cases. Should the Court continue to develop the line of reasoning used in *Adderley v. Florida*, the end result will be that the right of assembly and petition will become second-class rights. In the *Adderley* case, a group of Florida A & M students, disturbed by the arrest of a number of their classmates, assembled in front of the jail in Leon County. When they failed to disperse on orders of the sheriff, they were arrested for trespassing with malicious and mischievous intent. The Court upheld the convictions in a 5 to 4 decision. Justice Hugo L. Black, speaking for the majority, stated: "The State, no less than a private owner of property, has the power to preserve the property under its control for the use to which it is lawfully dedicated."[13] Extend that principle any further, say in a hostile community, and one would be lucky to speak in his own living room.

If we recognize that speech and action are both forms of conduct, then the expression test begins by examining the context in order to determine the essential or dominant quality of the conduct. If advice or persuasion is dominant, then it is expression and is thus protected by the First Amendment. If the emphasis is on instructions or preparations, then the conduct would, according to Emerson, be called action and would be subject to government regulations meeting due process requirements. As stated by Professor Emerson: "The essential task would be to distinguish between simply conveying an idea to another person, which idea he may later act upon; and actually participating with him in the performance of an illegal act."[14] Such a test, of course,

[10]Thomas Emerson, *The System of Freedom of Expression*, Random House, New York, 1970, pp. 17–20.
[11]*Yates v. United states*, 354 U.S. 298 (1957).
[12]For example, *Giboney v. Empire Storage and Ice Co.*, 336 U.S. 490 (1949).
[13]*Adderley v. Florida*, 385 U.S. 39, 47 (1966).
[14]*System of Freedom of Expression*, p. 75.

does not offer automatic solutions but rather is the beginning point in post facto analysis.

THE HOSTILE AUDIENCE: SKOKIE AND THE NAZIS

The Village of Skokie, Illinois, is located about 30 miles north of Chicago. It had a population in 1977 of 70,000, of whom approximately 40,000 were Jewish. Several thousand of the Jewish residents of Skokie were either survivors of Nazi concentration camps or surviving members of families that were murdered or imprisoned in the Nazi camps. Thus, in 1977, for many Skokie residents the horror of the Nazi holocaust remained a painful memory. The sight of the Nazi Swastika or a storm trooper's uniform aroused feelings of outrage among those who had witnessed the attempted genocide of European Jews. For those who cherished civilized values, the specter of Nazis marching in Skokie was an affront that could not go unchallenged. In some sense Frank Collin must have recognized this; indeed he may have relished the idea, as he made plans to demonstrate in this Chicago suburb.

In 1977 Frank Collin was the leader of the Chicago-based National Socialist party of America, a party described by Collin as a Nazi party. As the leader of a ragtag band of neo-Nazis, Collin probably knew that his unacceptable views of blacks and Jews would not receive serious public consideration unless he could manipulate the press and the courts, and for a number of years he was quite successful in doing just that. His immediate goal appears to have been to hold a Nazi rally in Marquette Park in Chicago, but he had been unsuccessful in obtaining the necessary permit from the Chicago Park District, which insisted that he obtain a large liability and property damage insurance policy.[15] Failing in this effort, Collin apparently decided on a ploy; instead of a rally in Chicago, he would hold one in the heart of the suburb of Skokie, a move that would be viewed by many as a deliberate and willful attempt to enrage the sensitivities of Skokie's large Jewish population. If that was his intent, he was successful. The Village of Skokie and the organized Jewish community reacted in some rather predictable ways. To obtain the necessary permit Collin was required to procure $350,000 in insurance. He then sent the Village a notice that the party intended to hold a peaceable public assembly to protest the insurance requirement; the marchers would be few in number, but they intended to wear their storm trooper uniforms, including the hated swastika armband. The Village obtained a restraining injunction. Throughout the nation public opinion rallied in support of the Village. After all, why should such a rag-tag group of outsiders be allowed to use the public facilities of Skokie in order to preach the morally reprehensible message of racial and religious hatred? Furthermore, the threat of violence was more than a remote possibility.

The outrage of the community was immediate; large counterdemonstrations were planned, and one witness estimated that as many as

[15]Cf. *Collin v. Chicago Park District*, 460 F.2d 746 (1972).

15,000 demonstrators would appear if the Nazis were allowed to enter Skokie. Few doubted the estimate. Why should a city with a large Jewish population be required to allow a demonstration that seemed calculated to arouse unrest, ill-will, and even violence? To stretch the First Amendment to protect Collin and his followers would appear to suggest that insulting, provocative, even irresponsible behavior has constitutional stature. Indeed, freedom of expression would seem to presume that its claimants will recognize certain outer limits to the rights of expression. Lastly, it must seem dubious to suggest that the Constitution would require the taxpayers of Skokie to pay, in effect, for a message they clearly did not want to hear. The added police personnel that might be required to maintain order could amount to a substantial cost for a small city. Indeed, what Skokie was being asked to do was to foot the bill in Collin's running battle with the Chicago Park District.

Yet money was not the real issue; the real issue was whether a community's threatened hostility to a morally repugnant view could prevail over an individual's right to express such views. The odds against Collin were substantial. To defend him would give the appearance of a tacit endorsement to the genocide of millions of Jews in Hitler's Germany and of Collin's advocacy of the expatriation of American blacks to Africa. The Chicago office of the American Civil Liberties Union, David Goldberger, attorney, chose to defend the unpopular cause. With little regard to the disaffection such a move would cause among its members and contributors, and to the probable negative consequences on its other litigation priorities, the ACLU placed its limited resources at the service not of Frank Collin but rather in defense of freedom of speech and assembly. If Collin and his small band of followers could be kept out of Skokie, then every unpopular view could be held in bondage by the threat of community violence. It is one thing to say that the state has a right to punish those who breach the peace or even those who provoke others to breach the peace, and quite another thing to say that the power of injunction can be used to stop a demonstration in advance, even though the demonstrators have given assurance that they will conduct themselves in a peaceful manner, in full cooperation with reasonable police instructions.[16] To allow such a degree of community advance control over speech and assembly would be prior restraint with a vengeance! It might well be appropriate to allow a restraining order in the context of immediate community violence or where there is evidence that potential demonstrators have a prior record of violent behavior. Such was not the case in Skokie. The only notes of violence were the threats made by local and national groups against allowing Collin to appear in uniform with the swastika armband. They claimed that their hostility to Nazi views was so deep and strong that the appearance of the Nazis would lead to violence.

The injunctions obtained by the Village were subsequently lifted,[17] but the government then proceeded to enact a series of ordinances aimed directly at the proposed demonstration. In part the ordinances:

---

[16]See *Village of Skokie v. National Socialist Party*, 366 N.E.2d. 347, 350 (1977).
[17]*National Socialist Party v. Village of Skokie*, 97 S.Ct. 2205 (1977).

1 required a permit for all parades or public assemblies of more than fifty persons and $350,000 in liability insurance

2 made it a punishable offense to intentionally disseminate any material inciting hatred against persons by reason of race, national origin, or religion and including within the ban the dissemination of posters, signs, handbills, or the public display of markings and clothing of symbolic significance.

3 prohibited public demonstration by members of political parties while wearing military-style uniforms

These ordinances effectively precluded the proposed May 1977 demonstration. Collin again sued the Village of Skokie. In the meantime he made plans for an April 20, 1978 rally in Skokie to celebrate the birthday of Adolph Hitler. Again counterdemonstrations were planned, and as the time approached the governor of Illinois proclaimed a Holocaust Remembrance Week and the Illinois legislature considered special legislation to bar the demonstration.

In late May of 1978 a federal court declared the ordinances unconstitutional[18] and Collin rescheduled his rally. However, the Skokie rally never took place because Collin was, in the meantime, successful in obtaining an order from a federal district court requiring the Chicago Park District to issue a permit for Marquette Park without the required insurance provision. Thus the Skokie rally did take place, but in Marquette Park in Chicago in July of 1978. Twenty-five members of the National Socialist party were escorted in police vans to the park, where they were protected by four hundred riot-helmeted police. They were met by two thousand counterdemonstrators who pelted them with rocks and eggs and shouted "Death to the Nazis."

The Skokie and Marquette Park cases raise several constitutional issues, two of which will be treated here. First is the problem of the hostile audience, either potential, as in Skokie, or actual. In the Skokie situation the initial response of the Village was to obtain an injunction, restraining in advance the proposed Nazi demonstration. In that context the Village argued that an uncontrollably violent situation would develop if Collin was allowed to demonstrate. The Village introduced several witnesses who supported this contention. The Village, in effect, was saying that it is more sensible to quell a speaker than to quell a mob. In the face of threats of chaos, bedlam, and violence, the Village sought a form of protective silencing. Yet the Supreme Court has repeatedly indicated that prior restraints are presumptively invalid and there is a heavy burden on the government to justify them.[19] Indeed in *Carroll v. President and Commissioners of Princess Anne* the Court struck down an injunction in a context not too dissimilar from Skokie.[20] In the *Princess Anne* case an injunction had been issued after a white-supremacist rally had been held and plans made for its continuation the next night. At the rally the speakers used deliberately derogatory, insulting, and threatening language aimed primarily at Jews and Negroes. The Court did not challenge the proposition that there might be special, limited circum-

---

[18]*Collin v. Smith*, 578 F.2d. 1197 (1978).
[19]For example, *New York Times v. United States*, 410 U.S. 713 (1971).
[20]393 U.S. 175 (1968).

stances in which speech might be unprotected because it was inter-laced with "burgeoning violence."[21] Yet the Court said that:

> Ordinarily, the State's constitutionally permissible interests are adequately served by criminal penalties imposed after freedom to speak has been so grossly abused that its immunity is breached. The impact and consequences of subsequent punishment for such abuse are materially different from those of prior restraint. Prior restraint upon speech suppresses the precise freedom which the First Amendment sought to protect against abridgment.[22]

What Collin proposed to do was deliberately provocative. The very presence of the Nazis in Skokie, in an area known to be "Jewish turf," would have been an insulting act calculated to arouse ill-will if not violence. Yet the scheme was not even the kind of imminent incitement to lawless action that could have arguably justified some post hoc punishment.[23] What the Village of Skokie had attempted to do was to censor ideas in advance of their presentation. In a free society that is a function of the individual, not the state. Unless the ideas penetrate some zone of constitutional privacy, for example, the home, the state should allow the individual the freedom to reject or "tune-out and turn-off" objectionable ideas.

A somewhat different problem emerges when a speaker actually confronts a hostile audience. Assuming for the moment that the Skokie rally had in fact taken place and the counterdemonstrators made their predicted appearance, would the Village then have been in a position to stop the rally, to punish Collin if he refused to cooperate? Clearly the First Amendment is not intended to protect incitement to riot. Thus if a speaker passes the boundary of expression and enters the area of calls to action—for example, incitement to riot or directing "fighting words" at particular members of the audience[24]—the state is no longer constrained by the First Amendment. Yet the mere threat of violence or turmoil by the audience, without more, would not justify denying a speaker his or her constitutional right of freedom of speech and assembly. Thus in *Cooper v. Aaron* the Court refused to allow a city to suspend the right of black students to attend nonsegregated schools merely because desegregation might cause violence.[25] Listeners are under some obligation to respect the rights of speakers, and in virtually all jurisdictions they are obligated under the criminal law to refrain from violence. To maintain otherwise would be tantamount to holding that those who have deep-seated and diametrically opposed views can never meet side-by-side to air their views since one side could veto the other's right of expression by muttering threats of chaos and turmoil.

One must concede that the line between a speaker's rights and the authority of the state to forestall a riot or other breaches of the peace is

---

[21]Ibid., p. 180; see also *Feiner v. New York*, 340 U.S. 1 (1949); cf. *Terminiello v. Chicago*, 337 U.S. 1 (1949).

[22]393 U.S. at 180–181.

[23]See *Brandenburg v. Ohio*, 395 U.S. 444 (1969).

[24]See ibid., and *Chaplinsky v. New Hampshire*, 315 U.S. 568 (1942).

[25]358 U.S. 1, 13 (1958).

necessarily difficult to draw, and in such a situation the police may be tempted to err on the side of public safety.[26] The police need to realize, however, that providing an outlet for views can have a stabilizing effect; that erring on the side of public safety may, in the long run, be short-sighted.

However unworthy the ideas of Frank Collin may be or however staged to attract the media, the fact is that Collin's proposed conduct was clearly to be an exercise in expression, not action. The First Amendment is intended to provide a process for expressing dissent. Whether expression has value should not depend on whether the state allows expression to take place but rather on the assessment of free individuals. As Justice Jackson once observed, " . . . every person must be his own watchman for truth."[27] Most certainly the value of expression should not depend on the willingness of listeners to restrain any urges to violence.

SYMBOLIC SPEECH

Foreigners to our shores have often been perplexed by the peculiar Yankee devotion to a piece of cloth dyed red, white, and blue. Yet "Old Glory" has been extolled for generations as the embodiment of all the national virtues, real or imagined. Every state in the union and the federal government have laws protecting the flag. But John Philip Sousa and Francis Scott Key aside, it had become high camp by the early 1970s to use the flag in ways that did not necessarily reflect the values of sacrifice, valor, and patriotism. During the Vietnam war it became incresingly popular to associate the flag with the trident peace symbol. It was not unnatural, under the circumstances, for many people to become outraged by what they believed to be the misuse, even desecration, of an honored symbol. Prosecutions under federal and state flag-misuse laws increased dramatically. The case of Harold Spence is only one of many. The difference, however, was that Spence was able to get his case reviewed by the United States Supreme Court.[28]

The Supreme Court, in a divided decision, reversed Spence's conviction under the improper-use statute of Washington. The majority characterized the case as being prosecution for the expression of an idea through activity. Even though no words were spoken or printed matter used, the majority ruled that Spence's act was a plain and peaceful expression of an idea, accomplished on private property, and that under these circumstances the state had no interest in preserving the physical integrity of a privately owned flag. Since Spence was not charged under a desecration statute, the majority refused to rule on whether the government has any valid interest in preserving the flag as a national symbol.

While the *Spence* opinion was carefully hedged by noting that the context of Spence's conduct was peaceful and that the privately owned flag was displayed on private property, the majority did accept that freedom of speech is broad enough to cover conduct that is nonverbal. Although the opinion did not even cast doubt on the prior two-level theory,

---

[26]For example, *Gregory v. Chicago*, 394 U.S. 111 (1969).
[27]Concurring in *Thomas v. Collins*, 323 U.S. at 545 (1945).
[28]*Spence v. Washington*, 94 S.Ct. 2727 (1974).

speech and speech plus cases, nonetheless the ruling stakes out a common-sense claim that symbolic conduct is often a means of expressing an idea.

The case of Harold Spence raises an interesting First Amendment question: Does freedom of speech and press cover only the spoken and written forms of communication, or does the amendment cover conduct intended to communicate ideas? In the Vietnam context this question was first raised in the *O'Brien* case in 1968.[29] In what was an act of protest against the draft and the war, O'Brien had burned his Selective Service registration card on the steps of the South Boston Courthouse. He was charged and convicted under a 1965 act for knowingly destroying his certificate. The conviction and the statute were upheld by the Supreme Court, which reasoned that the government had a substantial interest in ensuring the continued availability of Selective Service certificates and the legislation was a narrow means of protecting this interest, and further that the legislation reached only the noncommunicative impact of O'Brien's act.

First, there is some evidence to suggest that the 1965 legislation was passed by Congress not to protect a legitimate governmental interest, but rather to silence a particular symbolic form of dissent. Second, the context of O'Brien's arrest suggest that the arresting FBI agents were monitoring dissent rather than ensuring that all draft-age males, dissenters and orthodox believers alike, continued to preserve their draft cards.

Of course, O'Brien's conduct had the element of action, but the essence of his conduct was the expression of dissent. There is some element of physical action to all forms of expression. The question is whether the dominant feature is the expression of an idea or action.

One year after the *O'Brien* case the Court again had the issue of symbolic speech before it. In the *Tinker* case the majority upheld the right of Tinker, a high school student, to wear a black armband to school as a protest against the Vietnam war. The majority opinion reasoned that in the absence of any disruptive or potentially disruptive conduct, the act of wearing an armband as a protest was akin to "pure speech" and thus protected by the First Amendment.[30]

Does the *Tinker* case, however, resolve the swastika armband problem in the *Collin* case? A black armband would not be viewed as an unspeakable obscenity nor would it be likely to inflict psychic trauma on anyone, and finally, few would construe a black armband as a libel against a group. A swastika could arguably be banned on any of these grounds. Yet the swastika is a symbol of an idea, however false, just as the black armband in *Tinker* was a symbol of an idea. False ideas and their symbols need competition, not suppression. True, the swastika could inflict psychic trauma on a holocaust survivor, but that would suggest the need for an individual tort remedy, not suppression. As to the argument that a swastika is an obscenity and thus without social value, we need only pause a moment to realize that the logic of that argument could be extended to every unpopular or hated idea—abortion

[29]*United States v. O'Brien*, 391 U.S. 367 (1968).
[30]*Tinker v. Des Moines Independent School District*, 393 U.S. 503 (1969).

for instance. Finally, the argument that the swastika is a libel against Jews is equally unsound. Over a quarter of a century ago the Supreme Court did uphold a so-called group libel law,[31] primarily on the basis that religious and racial "libel" or bigotry caused violence. Such a dubious constitutional ruling should not be extended. In any event it would be difficult to apply the 1952 group libel ruling to a symbol, at least in the absence of proof of intent to injure.[32]

The *O'Brien* case allows the state to restrict symbolic speech in those situations where the government can prove a substantial interest unrelated to the suppression of free expression and where there is a connection between the proven interest and the restriction. In *Collin* there was a clear and important government interest in preventing violence and arguably a connection between this interest and the swastika. Yet if the government had the power to ban all symbols that have the potential for causing antisocial behavior, the list would be endless, including religious symbols, peace symbols, red flags, and black panthers, to name but a few. Thus, in 1978 Texas Tech University attempted to ban the wearing of masks by the Union of Iranian Students in an anti-Shah demonstration. The university argued that the masks encouraged violent activity by demonstrators, even though the masks had become a symbol of opposition to the Shah's regime.[33]

Preventing violence is an important government responsibility, and the government is not without power to accomplish this goal. A strong show of police force and the arrest and punishment of violent demonstrators are thought to have both a calming and a deterrent effect on would-be violators of the criminal laws.

THE TWO-LEVEL THEORY OF SPEECH

While the results were quite different, the *O'Brien* and *Tinker* cases share a common position that the First Amendment protects "pure speech" more than it does "speech plus." Justice Goldberg rationalized the two-level theory as follows:

The rights of free speech and assembly, while fundamental in our democratic society, still do not mean that everyone with opinions or beliefs to express may address a group at any public place and at any time. The constitutional guarantee of liberty implies the existence of an organized society maintaining public order, without which liberty itself would be lost in the excesses of anarchy. The control of travel on the streets is a clear example of governmental responsibility to insure this necessary order. A restriction in that relation, designed to promote the public convenience in the interest of all, and not susceptible to abuses of discriminatory application, cannot be disregarded by the attempted exercise of some civil right which, in other circumstances, would be entitled to protection. One would not be justified in ignoring the familiar red light because this was thought to be a means of

[31]*Beauharnais v. Illinois*, 343 U.S. 250 (1952).
[32]See *Gertz v. Welch*, 418 U.S. 323 (1974).
[33]*Aryan v. Mackey*, 462 F. Supp. 90 (1978).

social protest. Nor could one, contrary to traffic regulations, insist upon a street meeting in the middle of Times Square at the rush hour as a form of freedom of speech or assembly. Governmental authorities have the duty and responsibility to keep their streets open and available for movement. A group of demonstrators could not insist upon the right to cordon off a street, or entrance to a public or private building, and allow no one to pass who did not agree to listen to their exhortations. We emphatically reject the notion urged by appellant that the First and Fourteenth Amendments afford the same kind of freedom to those who would communicate ideas by conduct such as patrolling, marching, and picketing on streets and highways, as these amendments afford to those who communicate ideas by pure speech.[34]

This two-level theory incorrectly assumes that conduct can be precisely divided into pure expression, which receives the full protection of the amendment, and the expression plus action, which must be balanced against other social interests.

The two-level theory was again applied in 1969 in the Street case.[35] Street was convicted under a New York flag-misuse law. On June 6, 1966 Street, a black resident of Brooklyn, responded to the shooting of civil rights leader James Meredith by taking his American flag to a street corner and burning it. When the police arrived he was talking loudly to about thirty persons and was reported to have said, "We don't need no damn flag. . . . If they let that happen to Meredith we don't need an American flag."[36] His conviction was reversed in a 5 to 4 decision. The majority argued that his words were protected, and since the words were a part of the trial record it was possible that they may have unconstitutionally contributed to his conviction. Implicit in the reasoning was the assumption that if Street's act of burning the flag had not been accompanied by words it would have been examined in a different light. The majority did say, however, that there was a constitutional right to express one's opinion about the flag, including even contemptuous opinions. But the majority specifically refused to pass on the issue of whether a state could legally convict a person for the mere fact of burning the flag.

However, during the same year as the Spence case the Court handed down another flag-misuse case that strongly suggested that a narrowly drafted misuse statute could pass constitutional muster. In Smith v. Goguen a majority of the Court reversed the conviction of Goguen for wearing a small cloth flag sewn to the seat of his pants. He had been convicted under a Massachusetts law that made it a criminal offense to treat the flag with contempt. The conviction was reversed, not on First Amendment grounds, but because the statutory language was void for vagueness. In ruling that the phrase "treat contemptuously" was void for vagueness, the opinion did imply that a narrowly drafted flag-

---

[34]Cox v. Louisiana, 379 U.S. 536, 554; see also Gregory v. City of Chicago, 394 U.S. 111 (1969).

[35]Street v. New York, 394 U.S. 576.

[36]Ibid., p. 579.

misuse statute, such as the present federal act, which limits its reach to willful physical acts of desecration, would be acceptable.[37]

CONCLUSION

Protest and dissent often operate on the borderline of disorder. Yet the preservation of the right to dissent, even in volatile circumstances, is an important political and legal goal. The civil rights movement as well as the anti-Vietnam war protests often operated in volatile circumstances that threatened domestic tranquility. If freedom of expression for civil rights workers and anti-Vietnam protestors had been dependent on the sufferance of the government, it seems likely that in many locales it would never have been allowed. As the Supreme Court said in a 1969 civil rights case, a "municipality may not empower its licensing officials to roam essentially at will, dispensing or withholding permission to speak, assemble, picket, or parade, according to their own opinions regarding the potential effect of the activity in question."[38] It may seem strained to compare a Martin Luther King Jr. with a Frank Collin, yet once the law accords the government the right to keep a Collin out of Skokie, tomorrow's Martin Luther Kings will be denied public forums in the very communities where their protests are most needed.

[37]*Smith v. Goguen*, 94 S.Ct. 1242 (1974).
[38]*Shuttlesworth v. City of Birmingham*, 394 U.S. 147, 153 (1969).

CHURCH-STATE RELATIONS AND FREEDOM OF RELIGIOUS EXERCISE

4

There was once a time when America was rural, sober, Sabbatarian, and sanctified. It was the Golden Age of Protestantism, when, to borrow Robert M. Hutchins's phrase, "the good news of damnation" was carried to young and old. Today in urban America the good news is still around, and there are even some sober and Sabbatarian, perhaps even sanctified, pockets left; but the religious consensus that dominated the American scene throughout the nineteenth and well into the twentieth century has passed. In 1851, United States Supreme Court Justice Joseph Story could write: "Now there will probably be found few persons in this or any other Christian country, who would deliberately contend that it was unjust or unreasonable to foster and encourage the Christian religion, generally, as a matter of sound policy as well as a revealed truth."[1] Forty years later, Justice Joseph P. Bradley, in writing one of the Supreme Court's opinions on polygamy in the Utah Territory, spoke as if Christianity were a part of the nation's fundamental law: "The organization of a community for the spread and practice of polygamy is, in a measure, a return to barbarism. It is contrary to the spirit of Christianity and the civilization which Christianity has produced in the Western World"[2] Indeed, as recently as 1952, Justice William O. Douglas wrote in a majority opinion, "We are a religious people whose institutions presuppose a Supreme Being."[3]

To many persons in America today these statements have passed from hallowed to hollow. In a 1957 Gallup Poll, only 14 percent of those questioned responded that religion was losing its influence on American life. In response to the same question in 1970, 75 percent of the respondents thought religion was losing its influence.[4] The Gallup Poll has also reported a slow but steady decline in church attendance in America. In a 1949 poll, 49 percent of those questioned indicated that they had attended church within the past seven days. By 1969, that figure had declined to 42 percent.[5] For the majority of Americans, God is not dead;[6]

---

[1]Joseph Story, *Commentaries on the Constitution*, Little, Brown, Boston, 1851, vol. II, p. 592.
[2]*Latter Day Saints v. United States*, 136 U.S. 1 (1890).
[3]*Zorach v. Clauson*, 343 U.S. 306, 313 (1952).
[4]*Gallup Opinion Index*, no. 57, March 1970, p. 20.
[5]Ibid., no. 55, January 1970, p. 5.
[6]See ibid., no. 44, February 1969.

but there has been a decline in traditional forms of commitment to religious institutions.[7]

Of interest to students of government is that the passage of the Protestant era and the gradual decline of religious orthodoxy may well signify a new pattern of church-state relations in America. While the United States has been free of major church-state showdowns, a degree of tension has marked the relationship, particularly in the area of education. What may appear as paradoxical is that concurrently with the decline in orthodox religious commitment, public attitudes toward governmental financing of parochial education appear to have relaxed, a trend not necessarily reflected in the decisions of the Supreme Court.

CHURCH-STATE RELATIONS: THREE TRADITIONS

In the current controversy over church-state relations, the key phrase is "absolute separation of church and state." Yet it is worth recalling that separation of church and state is not a phrase lifted out of the Constitution, and it has only recently become a constitutional pillar. How absolute the separation should be is still an open question.

The colonial and Revolutionary periods in America produced three main traditions in church-state relations. These are the traditions of John Cotton, representative of the Puritan belief in an established church, of Roger Williams, the pious churchman who opposed establishment, and of Thomas Jefferson, a deist and skeptic who advocated a wall of separation between church and state.

Establishment   Few of the colonial settlers came to America with any intention of rejecting the idea of an established church. While there was little colonial support for a theocracy, there was general support in most of the Colonies for a state-supported church. John Cotton, one of Boston's great Puritan ministers, wrote in 1636:

> It is suitable to Gods all-sufficient wisdome and to the fulnes and perfection of Holy Scriptures, not only to prescribe perfect rules for the right ordering of a private man's soule to everlasting blessedness with himselfe, but also for the right ordering of a man's family, yea of the commonwealth too, so farre as both of them are subordinate to spiritual ends.[8]

The core of the Puritan philosophy in church-state relations is contained in those few lines: The word of God is clear and explicit, the civil state must accommodate itself to the will of God, and the will of God requires all men to subordinate themselves to spiritual ends. What this meant in practice was an established church. At the close of the colonial period, nine of the thirteen colonies had established churches. Yet establishment meant more than a state-supported church; it meant the close union of the church and state in social and religious endeavors.

[7]See generally Rodney Stark and Charles Glock, *American Piety: The Nature of Religious Commitment*, University of California Press, Berkeley and Los Angeles, 1968.
[8]Perry Miller and Thomas Johnson, *The Puritans*, American Book Co., New York, 1938, p. 209.

Nonetheless, other forces at work during the colonial period weakened the Puritan position. The growing diversity of Protestant sects made the position of a Cotton impractical. Religious pluralism became an important factor in the movement away from the twins of establishment and religious toleration to disestablishment and religious liberty.

Disestablishment   Roger Williams of Rhode Island pointed in the direction of the future pattern of church-state relations in America when he wrote: "All Civil States with their officers of justice in their respective constitutions and administrations . . . essentially Civill, and therefore not Judges, Governours or Defendeurs of the Spirituall or Christian State and Worship"[9] Williams was a champion of religious liberty and disestablishment. While John Cotton saw the church and state as partners in the cause of God's truth, Roger Williams believed that spiritual truth was so rare that it should not be tied to the state. Rhode Island, under the leadership of Williams, and Pennsylvania and Delaware had no established churches. Williams maintained that all churches should exist on an equal footing and all individuals be allowed liberty of conscience.

By the end of the colonial period, religious liberty for all Protestant sects was the accepted pattern. This shift from toleration to liberty carried with it a general loosening of church-state ties, but it had not resulted in any wholesale move for disestablishment. Disestablishment was a movement of the Revolutionary period. By the end of the Revolution, a majority of the states had effectively abolished state churches. But final disestablishment did not come until 1833 in Massachusetts.

The federal government, as distinct from the new state governments, began without an established church; and when the Bill of Rights was adopted, it contained a clause prohibiting Congress from enacting any law respecting an establishment of religion or prohibiting the free exercise of religion. But this limitation applied only to the national government until the 1930s, when the Supreme Court interpreted the due process clause of the Fourteenth Amendment as embodying the same limitations on the states.[10]

While separation of church and state was largely accomplished in the states by the end of the eighteenth century, disestablishment did not mean complete separation. Many states, as yet unrestricted by any federal limitation, continued well into the nineteenth century to actively cooperate with and aid various Protestant sects. Thus as late as 1852 New Hampshire retained in its constitution a permissive clause allowing local public support of Protestant religious instruction. Nor did religious liberty in the Revolutionary period and in the early years of the Republic mean full political rights for non-Protestants. Both Catholic and Jew suffered numerous civil limitations. The colonial settlers and their grandchildren had a deep suspicion of Catholics; and, while freedom of worship was allowed, both Catholics and Jews were frequently disfranchised and disqualified from public office by the states. New Jersey,

---

[9]Quoted in Clinton Rossiter, *Seedtime of the Republic*, Harcourt, Brace & World, New York, 1953, p. 197.
[10]*Hamilton v. Board of Regents*, 293 U.S. 245 (1934).

North Carolina, and New Hampshire did not drop anti-Catholic political limitations until the middle of the nineteenth century.

Separation   Disestablishment began to take on the modern overtones of separation in Virginia in the late eighteenth century. Under the leadership of James Madison and Thomas Jefferson, disestablishment began to mean a true severing of relations between church and state.

Jefferson's "wall of separation"   While Roger Williams had approached separation out of a pious distrust of the state, Jefferson approached separation out of fear of churches and an abiding skepticism of supernaturalism. It was Jefferson who coined the phrase a "wall of separation between church and state." In 1801, President Jefferson was requested by the Danbury Baptists Association to proclaim a day of fasting in connection with the nation's past ordeals. Both Washington and Adams had made similar proclamations. Jefferson refused and instead wrote the Danbury group:

> Believing with you that religion is a matter which lies solely between man and his God; that he owes account to none other for his faith or his worship; that the legislative powers of the Government reach actions only, and not opinions,—I contemplate with sovereign reverence that act of the whole American people which declared that their legislature should "make no law respecting an establishment of religion, or prohibiting the free exercise thereof," thus building a wall of separation between Church and state.[11]

By the middle of the twentieth century, the no-establishment clause of the First Amendment has been all but forgotten, and in its place Jefferson's phrase had been substituted, but with an absolutism that Jefferson had never intended. As an eighteenth-century deist, Jefferson did not advocate absolute separation. For example, in the field of public education Jefferson was opposed to denominational control or influence, but he believed that the common core of religion should be included. In his draft of a statute to establish a public school system in Virginia, Jefferson merely held that there should be "no religious reading, instruction or exercise . . . inconsistent with the tenets of any religious sect or denomination."[12] Still, even Jefferson's nonabsolutist theory of separation was too advanced for his era. As long as Protestantism retained an overwhelming consensus in America, the Protestant churches and the states continued a lively partnership.

The Protestant Crusade   When the Republic was established in 1789, the Catholic population numbered 35,000, with approximately twenty-five priests led by Bishop John Carroll. By 1822, the Catholic population had increased to about 100,000. With the coming of the great Irish and German migrations of the 1840s and 1850s, the Catholic population

[11] Quoted in Anson P. Stokes, *Church and State in the United States*, Harper & Row, New York, 1949, vol. II, p. 227.
[12] *The Writings of Thomas Jefferson*, Bergh Edition, Jefferson Memorial Association, Washington, D.C., 1907, vols. 17–18, p. 425.

reached 2 million. Anti-Catholicism, never far from the surface, now en-
gulfed a large portion of the nation. "No Popery" became the battle cry
of such men as Samuel F. B. Morse and the Reverend Lyman Beecher.
Catholic convents and churches were burned in New York, Boston, Philadelphia, and Newark. While the Protestant crusade of the 1840s and
1850s was as much antiforeign as it was anti-Catholic, nonetheless it
drove a deep wedge between Protestants and Catholics in America.

The Catholic population naturally resented the more vicious forms of
bias practiced by the Know-Nothings and the American Protestant Union.
The most sensitive area of conflict, then as now, was centered around
public education. When the great mass of Catholics arrived in the United
States, they found a public school system that was thoroughly Protestant
in all respects. Catholic children were required to read the Protestant
version of the Bible, sing Protestant hymns, and recite Protestant prayers;
and history was taught with a Reformation bias. The extent of this influence can be seen in New York City. A Protestant group known as the
Public School Society acquired a virtual monopoly of the public schools,
operating them with public funds. There was a secular movement in public
education, but even the most secular-minded of all educational leaders,
Horace Mann, considered indoctrination in the Christian religion a required part of public education. There is little doubt that Mann believed
that the Christian religion was equivalent to interdenominational Protestantism.

While it is likely that there would have been some type of parochial
school system, this Protestant domination of the public schools acceler-
ated the movement. At first the Catholics demanded a share of state
school funds to support Catholic schools. When this was rejected, the
Catholics responded with a drive for the parish parochial school and
increased their demands that the public schools become entirely secular in order to protect the Catholic children enrolled in them.

By the latter part of the nineteenth century and the early part of the
twentieth, American Catholics, under the leadership of Archbishops Ire-
land and Gibbons, were assimilating into the American pattern of church-
state relations. Above all, American Catholics accepted separation of
church and state and religious liberty; indeed the Catholic Church thrived
in America under separation. However, the Catholics had assumed an
enormous financial burden in the parochial school system. The time
would come when they would seek public assistance to relieve the burden.

THE PRACTICE OF SEPARATION

Bus transportation   In areas of high Catholic population, demands for
indirect financial relief for parents of parochial school children have
been made with increasing regularity within the past twenty-five years. A
frequent demand has been for bus transportation. In 1941, New Jersey
passed a permissive statute allowing local school districts to reimburse
the parents of all school children for bus transportation. When the parents
of parocial school children were given reimbursement, the law was attacked as a violation of separation of church and state. The attack
reached the Supreme Court in 1947.

In *Everson v. Board of Education*,[13] the Court took the opportunity to interpret "no establishment" in strong Jeffersonian terms. The Court stressed that neither a state nor the federal government must pass laws that aid one religion or all religions or prefer one religion over another. Nor may the government levy any tax to support any religious activity or institution. Still, the Court was unwilling to strike down the New Jersey bus law. Relying on the earlier "child benefit theory," the Court concluded that the bus was directed at the safety of the child and not to the benefit of a religion.

The child benefit theory had been used previously to uphold the constitutionality of a state law that provided free nonsectarian textbooks to all school children, parochial and public.[14] Textbooks and instructional materials are supplied to parochial students in fourteen states. Public bus transportation of parochial students prevails in hundreds of school districts in twenty-four states. Public health and welfare services are extended to parochial schools in fifteen states, and eleven states extend services to educationally disadvantaged students in church-related schools. Finally, in nine states some school districts allow parochial students to dual enroll for certain public school courses.

Religious observances and instruction   There is little question that the public school system is far more secular today than it was one hundred years ago. On the other hand, the system has never totally divorced itself from the American religious heritage. Bible readings, Christmas plays, prayers, and hymns are accepted practices in many areas of the United States. At one time, this was largely a Protestant influence, but as parochial schools lagged in development and more and more Catholic children attended public schools, the Catholics joined Protestant and Jewish groups in an effort to bring optional sectarian instruction into the public schools. This movement, known as the weekday church school program, began in 1914. One variant of the movement provided for the release of pupils duiring school hours to attend sectarian instruction within the school building. In 1948, the year following the bus transportation case, the United States Supreme Court had an opportunity to examine the released-time program.

In *McCollum v. Board of Education* the Court faced a situation in which pupils had the option of attending religious instruction in the classroom or going to a study hall. The instruction was given by outside religious teachers and no public funds were used for the immediate purpose of the program. The Court held this to be in violation of the no-establishment clause, primarily because it amounted to the use of tax-supported property for religious instruction, but also because of the close cooperation of the public school and the local religious council in promoting religion and because of the use of the compulsory education system to provide an audience for sectarian instruction.[15]

The *McCollum* decision was important, not so much because it struck down the released-time program, but rather because it was an indication

[13]*Everson v. Board of Education*, 330 U.S. 1 (1947).
[14]*Cochran v. Louisiana*, 281 U.S. 370 (1930).
[15]*McCollum v. Board of Education*, 333 U.S. 203 (1948).

of a growing sentiment of the Court, first noted in the *Everson* case, in favor of an absolutist position in church-state relations. Not only did the Court accept "no estabishment" as equivalent to a high wall of separation but also the Court interpreted the gradual elimination of particular sectarian domination of public schools to mean that public education should be exclusively secular in operation and orientation.

The weekday church school movement had widespread support from Catholics, Protestants, and Jews. The *McCollum* decision went too far. Within four years, in 1952, the Court limited the impact of its decision by upholding a New York program for the dismissal of public school children during school hours to receive religious instruction at designated centers away from the public school.[16] The main element in the *McCollum* decision which was absent in this new dismissed-time decision was the use of tax-supported property, but the other elements of cooperation and captive audience were present, and the majority of the Court chose to ignore them.

The dismissed-time program, while it has received some setbacks, is extensively practiced throughout the United States. In New York City alone, more than 100,000 children are excused one hour a week for religious instruction. In the face of this practice, to push the doctrine of separation too far could be construed as indicating a hostility toward religion. Our constitutional system presupposes no such hostility. Nor is there a practical argument against such a program. Certainly the argument of religious pluralism presents no barrier to such an off-campus option program. As the United States Supreme Court said in the New York dismissed-time case, "When the state encourages religious instruction or cooperation with religious authorities by adjusting the schedule of public events to sectarian needs, it follows the best of our traditions." The Constitution cannot be callous toward religion; if it were it would prefer the nonbeliever over the believer.[17] Yet an off-campus option for religious instruction would not justify giving academic credit to students for Bible study courses taken in a released-time program, especially where the program was geared to advancing sectarian beliefs.[18]

PUBLIC SCHOOL PRAYERS AND BIBLE READINGS

A Southern senator blasted, "They have taken God out of the schools and put the Nigras in." The occasion for this intemperance was a 1962 Supreme Court decision holding the New York State public school prayer unconstitutional. The brief and denominationally neutral prayer, a daily classroom exercise, read: "Almighty God, we acknowledge our dependence upon Thee, and we beg Thy blessing upon us, our parents, our teachers, and our Country."

In anticipation of adverse public reaction, the Court noted that to prohibit state laws respecting an establishment of religious services in the public schools did not indicate any hostility toward prayer or religion: "It is neither sacrilegious or antireligious to say that each separate govern-

[16]*Zorach v. Clauson*, 343 U.S. 306 (1952).
[17]Ibid., p. 305.
[18]See *Lanner v. Wimmer*, 463 F. Supp. 867 (1978).

ment in this country should stay out of the business of writing or sanctioning official prayers and leave that purely religious function to the people themselves and to those the people choose to look to for religious guidance."[19]

The reaction to the decision was loud and largely ill-considered. In Congress the decision was called "godless," and thirty constitutional amendments were introduced to reverse it. The proposed amendments had all the characteristics of token gestures of defiance to pacify constituents. The proposals died for lack of support in Congress.

The controversy did not end with the New York prayer case. In 1962, forty states and the District of Columbia used Bible readings and prayers as a regular part of public school exercises. Indeed, ten states even required by statute the recitation of prayers or Bible readings.[20] After the New York decision, public schools continued the recitation of prayers and the reading of selections from the Bible. Some of the schools justified this by contending that the Court had disallowed only officially composed prayers.

In 1963, the court disabused the public schools of this impression. In two companion state cases, the Court, in an 8 to 1 decision, declared that Bible readings and prayers in public schools were religious ceremonies in violation of the no-establishment clause as applied to the states by the due process clause of the Fourteenth Amendment.[21]

In one of the cases, a Pennsylvania law required the daily reading of at least ten Bible verses. The Edward Schempp family of Germantown brought an action against the law. The Schempps, as Unitarians, found the daily reading of the King James Bible and the recitation of the Lord's Prayer a trinitarian religious ceremony and as such contrary to their religious beliefs. The second case was instituted by an atheist Baltimore mother in behalf of her atheist son. The mother felt that religious ceremonies in the Baltimore schools placed a premium on belief as against nonbelief, thus making alien and sinister the moral values of the nonbeliever.

The 1953 decision was a return to the spirit of the *Everson* and *McCollum* decisions. In essence, the Court asserted that in the matter of religion the state must be neutral, neither advancing nor inhibiting religion. It recognized that religion has a place in public education but not as religious ceremony. The legitimate place of religion in education could only be through the study of comparative religion, religious history, or Biblical literary studies presented in a secular and objective manner. In conclusion, the Court observed that "the place of religion in our society is an exalted one, one achieved through reliance on the home, the church and the inviolable citadel of the individual heart and mind.

The immediate public reaction to the decision was mixed but more temperate than the reaction to the 1962 New York prayer case. The National Council of Churches, representing major Protestant leaders, felt that school prayers and Bible readings cheapened religion, particularly

[19]*Engel v. Vitale*, 370 U.S. 421 (1962).

[20]Donald E. Boles, *The Bible*, Religion, and the Public Schools, Iowa State University Press, Ames, 1961, chap. 2.

[21]*Murray v. Curlett* and *School District of Abington v. Schempp*, 83 S. Ct. 1580 (1963).

when used by school officials as a means of maintaining classroom discipline. The Synagogue Council of America, representing Orthodox, Conservative, and Reform Judaism, also approved of the Court's action. Roman Catholics, who one hundred years ago had fought against these very practices, were divided; but the weight of opinion was against the decision. Monsignor John Voight, secretary for education of the Roman Catholic archdiocese of New York, felt the decision was wrong because it would foster secularism in public education and because it ignored the wishes of a majority of parents who favored religious practices. In this he was joined by Bishop Fred P. Corson of the World Methodist Council.

It is probably true that majority opinion has supported Bible readings and prayers, and hence the Supreme Court could be accused of thwarting majority rule. Yet democracy is not a simple problem in arithmetic. Democratic majority rule must be balanced by respect for minority rights. One of the basic purposes of our Bill of Rights is to keep the majority from imposing a tyranny, religious or otherwise, on the minority.

The prayer and Bible-reading decisions: compliance   The big question after 1962 was whether such long-standing customs could be altered by judicial decisions. This author conducted a national random survey of public elementary-school teachers during the academic year 1964–65. The mail questionnaire was sent to 2,320 teachers and 1,712 responded. The results, as shown in Table 5, indicate that since the Court handed down its decision, there has been a noticeable shift in actual classroom practices.[22] While the data in the table indicate a significant national shift away from classroom prayers and Bible readings, the data also revealed that a majority of Southern respondents continued prayers and Bible readings. There has also been some isolated opposition in the North. In 1969, Illinois, Indiana, and New Jersey all enacted legislation permitting public schools to conduct brief periods of meditation or silent prayer. However, in 1969, a federal district court ruled a Pennsylvania school district's Bible reading and prayer policy in violation of the First Amendment.[23] A similar decision was reached in a 1970 New Jersey case.[24]

It is worth recalling that the Supreme Court observed in the *Schempp* decision that the academic study of religion was not precluded by the First Amendment. Justice Tom C. Clark, speaking for the majority, noted that the study of religion or the history of religion or the study of the historic and literary qualities of the Bible, if presented as an objective part of a secular program, would be consistent with the First amendment. Since 1963, at least three states—Nebraska, Pennsylvania, and Florida—have experimented with academic religious programs—programs designed as illumination rather than indoctrination.[25] On the other hand, sectarian Bible-study courses conducted in public schools clearly violate the no-

---

[22]Row totals in Table 5 do not equal 1,712 either because respondents did not answer a question or because they were not teaching before 1962.

[23]*ACLU v. Albert Gallatin School District*, 307 F.S. 637 (1969).

[24]*New Jersey State Board of Education v. Board of Education of Netcong*, 262 A.2d 21 (1970).

[25]See Edwin S. Gaustad, "Teaching about Religion in the Public Schools," *Journal of Church and State*, vol. 2, pp. 265–267, Spring 1969

establishment clause.[26] Similarly, courses offered by the public schools that are religious in their orientation, such as courses in transcendental meditation, would also come within the proscriptions of no establishment.[27]

TABLE 5   Classroom practices: prayers and Bible reading

Practice	Daily	Weekly	Less than weekly	Not at all
Morning prayers				
Before 1962	720	33	19	498
1964–1965	1321	24	29	946
Bible reading				
Before 1962	512	72	106	745
1964–1965	208	43	103	1261

GOVERNMENT AID TO SECTARIAN SCHOOLS: THE PROS AND CONS

The immigrant Roman Catholic Church assumed an enormous financial burden when it decided to undertake a parochial school system. As the burden became heavier, the Catholics requested assistance from the states. In turn, this drove a wedge between Catholics and supporters of a secular public school system. Some states responded by passing legislation indirectly aiding the parochial schools, such as free bus transportation and free secular textbook laws. However, these laws could not stem the tide of increasing educational costs.

The Catholic position: unequal burdens and equality of the law
Basically, the Catholic position on government aid is that Catholics are currently being denied natural or distributive justice in the double taxation imposed on them in educating their children. Catholics and non-Catholics alike agree that it is a constitutional, indeed, a natural right, of all parents to supervise the education of their children.[28] Some parents have chosen to exercise this right in public schools, and others have elected to send their children to schools that include religious training. There is nothing inherently logical in the position that because a minority have elected the state-operated school system, all the tax moneys for education must go to that system. Why should the Catholics forfeit their due share of the public funds which they contributed to and which have been set aside for education merely because they choose a different method of exercising the same constitutional right that the parents of public school children are exercising? It is clearly inequitable to place a penalty on the exercise of a constitutional right. No such penalty is found in Canada, Great Britain, Germany, Holland, or France, where the state does aid the church schools.

[26]See *Wiley v. Franklin*, 468 F. Supp. 133 (1979).
[27]See *Malnok v. Yogi*, 592 F.2d 197 (1979).
[28]*Pierce v. Society of Sisters*, 268 U.S. 510 (1925).

Catholics and other nonpublic-school supporters of governmental aid programs also stress that the melting-pot philosophy is hopelessly outdated. Nonpublic schools offer variety and diversity and constitute an important alternative choice to public schools. Educational pluralism enables large groups of Americans to continue to express themselves socially, ethnically, culturally, and religiously through diverse educational institutions. Finally, supporters of various aid programs stress that it is in the economic interest of the public to ensure the continued existence of nonpublic schools. They point out that the pattern of closing private schools increases enormously the costs to the local public school districts, particularly the urban, inner-city districts, and that these are the districts least able to assume added responsibilities. In the twenty largest cities in America about two out of five school children are enrolled in nonpublic schools. These cities, already overburdened with rising taxes and with a history of rejection of school bond issues, would be the hardest hit by further closing of parochial schools. Proponents stress that the tide of pupil transfers could easily topple inner-city districts already operating under severe fiscal constraints.[29]

The non-Catholic position   When the Roman Catholics point out that they are educating millions of elementary and secondary school children at a considerable financial sacrifice, the non-Catholic is apt to reply that the Catholics choose to make the sacrifice, that it is not imposed on them by the state. The American Civil Liberties Union stated the case thus:

> Every American is free to send his child or children to the public schools . . . or, alternatively, to send them to a church-controlled school. It has been urged in the name of "distributive justice" that parents who wish to send their children to religious schools are penalized for the "free exercise" of their religion. . . . But all citizens must be prepared to pay in one way or another for their convictions or preferences.

Still, the fact that a Catholic parent has a choice does not explain why the preference should carry an additional price.

There are a multitude of reasons why the non-Catholic expects the Roman Catholic to pay the additional price. The colonial heritage of anti-Catholicism still lingers on in America. There are suspicions among such groups as Protestants and Others United for Separation of Church and State about the political philosophy of the Catholic Church, about its seeming antidemocratic attitudes, and about its willingness to step into the political arena in obvious power-bloc moves. There is also a degree of religious rivalry and distrust, a fear by Protestants and Jews that any aid to the parochial school will further the strength of the Catholic Church in America, a strength they already fear. There is also a deep and abiding conviction that the parochial school system is a divisive element in our society and should not be encouraged. To many Americans, the public school is the place and indeed the best place for young Americans to learn about democracy, about social tolerance and class fluidity. Thus

[29]See President's Panel on Nonpublic Education, *Final Report*, 1972.

the non-Catholic, while willing to allow the parochial system to exist, does not feel that an institution that shields the child from competing ideologies and values should be developed with state funds.

A study conducted by the National Opinion Research Center at the University of Chicago concluded that Catholic-school Catholics are not more isolated than are coreligionists who did not attend Catholic schools. Nor are Catholic-school Catholics more rigid and intolerant than Catholics who attended public schools. Indeed, they were found to be more tolerant with regard to civil liberties and to possess greater social conciousness than Catholics of the same age and educational level who had not gone to Catholic schools. The study concluded that there were no traces of any divisive influences attributable to parochial education and that the charge that Catholic schools have a harmful influence on the social consensus of the nation was not supported by the data.[30]

Opponents of parochial-school-aid programs also point out that the decline in parochial school enrollments may not be simply the result of increased operating costs and consequent closing of schools. They suggest that the decline may also be the result of a choice by Catholic parents in favor of public education; that, in effect, these parents have voluntarily rejected the parochial schools. They also note that the economic threat of dumping large numbers of parochial students on the public schools may be an unloaded gun. Declining birth rates have now caught up with the public schools and overcrowding is not the serious threat it once was. Finally, the opponents argue that most aid programs conflict with the First Amendment policy of mutual abstention by church and state. Indeed, aid programs, they argue, will have a contrary effect on the policy of keeping politics out of religion and religion out of politics. In legislative halls across the nation an element of religious divisiveness will become an unfortunate but common feature of the annual appropriation process, as sectarian lobbyists press for increasingly higher levels of support for parochial schools.

THE SUPREME COURT AND
AID PROGRAM

Pressure for direct and indirect state aid to nonpublic schools increased rapidly in the mid-1960s. After passage of the federal Elementary and Secondary Education Act of 1965 many proponents of aid concluded that the political deadlock had ended and that the way was now open for the states to make significant contributions to the financially embattled parochial schools. They also concluded that the federal constitutional problems were no longer a major roadblock to financial aid. In this they were influenced by the Supreme Court's decision in 1968 in *Board of Education v. Allen*.[31] In the *Allen* case, Justice White, speaking for the majority, concluded that a 1965 New York law providing free secular textbooks to *all* school pupils did not contravene the no-establishment clause.

---

[30]Andrew Greeley and Peter Rossi, *The Education of Catholic Americans*, Aldine Publishing Co., Chicago, 1966, chap. 5.
[31]392 U.S. 236 (1968).

Justice White, the Court's strongest church-state accommodationist, reasoned that the New York law met the test of the *Schempp* case, that is, that the law had a valid secular legislative purpose and that the primary effect of the law was neither to advance nor to inhibit religion.[32] This twofold test became an alternative to the "no aid" position advanced by Justice Black in his 1947 *Everson* decision.[33]

The *Allen* case, however, was a weak reed on which to pin accommodationist hopes, because the six-justice majority contained two justices who were shortly to leave the Court, Warren retiring in 1969 and Harlan in 1971, and because two of the justices, Brennan and Marshall, were not committed to Justice White's accommodationist views. In any event, a number of states, among them Michigan, New York, Pennsylvania, Rhode Island, Connecticut, and Ohio, passed legislation in the late 1960s and early 1970s extending financial aid to sectarian schools. The aid was in the form of direct or indirect grants to the schools for the purchase of secular teaching services or indirect aid in the form of tuition grants, tax credits for parents, or payment for auxiliary services, such as mandated record keeping and testing.

The first review of these programs came in 1971 and involved the Rhode Island and Pennsylvania legislation. These state programs involved salary supplements paid to parochial school teachers who taught secular subjects and direct grants to parochial schools for the "purchase" of certain secular educational services. With only Justice White dissenting, the Court, speaking through the new Chief Justice, Warren Burger, struck down both statutes as violative of the no-establishment clause. Relying on the twofold test adopted in the *Schempp* case plus the no-excessive-entanglement test recently announced in the church tax-exemption case, the majority reasoned that while the legislation had a valid secular purpose, it was unnecessary to determine the primary effect of legislation since the programs failed the third test of excessive entanglement between government and religion. Acknowledging that in the abstract secular and religious education are separable and identifiable, the Chief Justice reasoned, somewhat paradoxically, that both states, in order to guard against subsidized teachers inculcating religion, would, of necessity, have to develop comprehensive, discriminating, and continuing state surveillance of subsidized teachers. "These prophylactic contacts will involve excessive and enduring entanglement between church and state."[34] In other words, in order to forestall a challenge under the rule against promoting religion and thus invalidating a program under the second test of the *Schempp* case, the state programs were invalidated instead under the third test, no excessive entanglement, because they did not fail the second test. As Justice White observed, that did seem to be an insoluble paradox.

Although the *Lemon* opinion offered no formula for the determination of excessive entanglement, the opinion did suggest that the goal of no excessive entanglement was to guard against political divisiveness and that direct grant programs, subject always to the annual legislative appropri-

[32]*Abington School District v. Schempp*, 374 U.S. 203 (1963).
[33]*Everson v. Board of Education*, 330 U.S. 1 (1947).
[34]*Lemon v. Kurtzman*, 403 U.S. 602, 619 (1971).

ation process, were potentially divisive. "Ordinarily political debate and division, however vigorous or even partisan, are normal, and healthy manifestations of our democratic system of government, but political division along religious lines was one of the principal evils against which the First Amendment was intended to protect. The political divisiveness of such conflict is a threat to the normal political process."[35]

Lemon v. Kurtzman did not, however, settle the issue of aid to nonpublic schools. Indeed a careful reading of the *Lemon* opinion suggests that the Chief Justice was keeping the door open to narrowly conceived indirect aid programs. In any event, no matter how firmly the door might have been closed, the *Lemon* opinion was not acceptable to large numbers of well-organized and politically skillful people, and they continued their efforts to devise legislation that would pass constitutional muster.

In 1971 and 1972 both Pennsylvania and New York enacted new aid programs. The legislation was immediately contested in the courts, reaching the Supreme Court in 1973. In *Committee for Public Education v. Nyquist*,[36] a six-justice majority struck down the New York legislation that extended direct maintenance and repair grants to sectarian schools, and offered tuition reimbursement, or a tax credit in lieu of tuition reimbursement, to parents of nonpublic school pupils.

Justice Powell's majority opinion in the New York case applied the same tests as were applied in the *Lemon* case, holding that all three programs failed the test against advancing religion. Looking behind the labels, his opinion stressed that the effect and substantive impact of the aid was to unmistakably provide desired support for sectarian institutions. And using a similar line of reasoning Justice Powell, again speaking for a six-justice majority, struck down the Pennsylvania tuition-grant legislation. Scorning the "indirect" and "direct" aid distinctions of previous cases, he again looked to the substantive impact, the practical effect, of the tuition legislation and concluded that the intended consequence of the legislation was to preserve and support religion-oriented institutions, and thus it failed the First Amendment test against promoting or advancing religion.[37]

The 1973 opinions raised substantial constitutional hurdles to any form of meaningful state aid to sectarian elementary and secondary education. While a majority of the justices were willing to allow some limited aid to the secular activities of church-related colleges,[38] state aid in the area of elementary and secondary parochial schools faced the prospect of serious court challenges. The 1973 decisions were not likely to convince proponents of aid programs that the issue had been settled, particularly in view of the divisions within the Court. The result has been a continuation of the effort to obtain state aid, either direct or indirect, for sectarian elementary and secondary schools. And the litigation continues. In 1975 in *Meek v. Pittinger*, a badly divided Court upheld portions of a Pennsylvania act that extended secular textbook loans to students

[35]Ibid., p. 622.
[36]93 S.Ct. 2955; in 1974 in *Franchise Tax Board v. United Americans*, a federal district court in California summarily struck down California's tax-credit plan for parents of nonpublic school children, and in October 1974 the Supreme Court affirmed this action without an opinion.
[37]*Sloan v. Lemon*, 93 S.Ct. 2982 (1973).
[38]See *Tilton v. Richardson*, 91 S.Ct. 209 (1971), and *Hunt v. McNair*, 93 S.Ct. 2868 (1973).

in sectarian schools, but the Court struck down sections of the act that extended other forms of aid to sectarian schools.[39] The latter provisions would have offered instructional materials, equipment, and certain auxiliary services to sectarian schools. The opinion reasoned that these materials and services would either directly benefit the religious enterprise or would at least require substantive state monitoring in order to ensure that the services did not advance religion. However, the *Meek* decision pointedly suggested in two footnotes that the issue of auxiliary services was still open, at least if the services were of a class of general welfare services in which only incidental benefit accrued to the church-related school.[40]

Meek was decided in 1975, and in the following year the Ohio legislature passed legislation that would have extended the following benefits to nonpublic pupils:

1 Loans of securlar textbooks

2 Testing and scoring services in secular subjects

3 Diagnostic services parallel to those available to public school pupils in the areas of speech, hearing, and psychological services conducted by public personnel on the premises of the nonpublic schools

4 Therapeutic psychological, speech, hearing, guidance, counseling, and remedial services and programs for the deaf, blind, emotionally disturbed, and physically handicapped; programs and services to be conducted off the nonpublic school premises or in mobile units by public personnel

5 Secular instructional materials and equipment loans to pupils or parents

6 Field trip transportation and services for enrichment of instruction in secular areas

The legislation was attacked as a violation of the no-establishment clause, and in 1977 the Supreme Court, in *Wolman v. Walter*, upheld the benefits contained in items 1–4 and struck down the portions dealing with instructional materials, equipment, and field trips.[41]

The *Wolman* decision goes further than any prior decision in extending secular aid to nonpublic school pupils. Although the opinion was divided and even subdivided, still there was a solid 8 to 1 majority favoring diagnostic services and a 7 to 2 majority supporting the various therapeutic services and programs. The textbook and testing sections were upheld by 6 to 3 splits. The majority was satisfied that the programs were secular, neutral, and would require no excessive state surveillance and consequently no impermissible state-church entanglement.[42]

Some obvious parallels could be drawn between secular textbooks and secular instructional materials and equipment. The fact that the Court supports the former and not the latter can only be explained by reference to a commitment that some justices on the *Wolman* majority have toward *stare decisis*.[43] Apparently there is no longer a majority that would

[39]421 U.S. 349.

[40]See footnotes 17 and 21, 421 U.S. at 368 and 371.

[41]433 U.S. 229.

[42]On this issue of excessive entanglement on a related matter, see *NLRB v. Catholic Bishop of Chicago*, 99 S.Ct. 1313 (1979).

[43]See footnote 18, 433 U.S. at 251.

support a secular textbook program loan if it were presented as an entirely new issue.

What then can we conclude from the somewhat seesaw course of these decisions? The first and perhaps most obvious conclusion is that the Court remains strongly opposed to any form of aid to nonpublic school pupils or parents that would be the functional equivalent of a cash grant in support of the secular instructional functions of sectarian schools. The only exception to this is the textbook loan program, a precedent that the majority has pointedly noted it will not expand. The second conclusion, however, is that there is now a substantial majority ranging in size from six to eight justices, that is willing to support religiously neutral noninstructional auxiliary services. The services must be of direct assistance to the pupils rather than the schools. The line that distinguishes the nonreligious needs of sectarian pupils from the normal financial obligations of religious schools is difficult to draw. Apparently the Court has settled on a line that denies sectarian schools any assistance in the discharge of the normal obligations associated with running a school, such as plant development and maintenance; administrative, clerical, and instructional salaries; and the purchase of supplies and equipment, however, religiously neutral. Religiously neutral auxiliary services, then, may be a part of an educational enterprise and may be supportive of the instructional component of the schools, but such services may not be a direct substitute for the necessary and normal obligations of a sectarian school. Doubtlessly this position will not satisfy those who believe that sectarian schools deserve and need greater state financial assistance. Furthermore, it is not the type of constitutional demarcation that will end dispute and litigation. The blurred lines between direct and indirect aid will necessarily produce a degree of tension. Yet a clear-cut line, one that either denied all aid to sectarian pupils or imposed no limits on aid, would be even less acceptable.

THE CHURCHES AND TAX EXEMPTION

During the colonial period, when churches were agencies of the state, it made a good deal of sense to exempt religious property from taxation. With the coming of disestablishment, while anticlericalism was not uncommon, the tradition of tax exemption survived. Of course, it survived as a matter of state grace and not as a constitutional right. It was questioned from time to time, and in 1875 President Grant went so far as to devote a congressional message to the issue. He cautioned that church property was becoming a burden on the tax structure and suggested "the taxation of all property equally, whether church or corporation, exempting only the last resting place of the dead, and possibly, with proper restrictions, church edifices."[44]

Church wealth   President Grant estimated that by 1875 church property in the United States was valued at $1 billion. This was probably an exaggeration, since the 1870 census listed church property at

[44]Quoted in Leo Pfeffer, *Church, State and Freedom*, rev. ed., Beacon Press, Boston, 1967, p. 216.

$354,483,581.[45] No available statistics can give an accurate account of current church wealth in the United States. That it is vast seems beyond dispute. In 1960, for example, sixty Protestant churches reported contributions totaling $3,266,533,260. There has been a steady growth in tax-exempt property. In 1931, it was estimated that 12 percent of all real estate was tax exempt. By 1961, the estimated figure was 31 percent. Approximately 5 percent of all tax-exempt property is owned by religious organizations. However, if public tax-exempt property is excluded, then the religious ownership proportion would be considerably higher.[46] In the early 1960s, Martin Larson conducted a study of tax-exempt property in four large cities. He estimated that the true value of all American real estate was $1,140 billion, and that of this, $80 billion was accounted for by religiously exempt property.[47] The increase in church wealth and the concurrent growth in government services and the consequent need for additional revenues made it inevitable that the question of tax exemption of church wealth and income be reexamined. As Eugene Carson Blake, then Stated Clerk of the United Presbyterian Church, said in 1959, "A government with mounting tax problems cannot be expected to keep its hands off the wealth of a rich church forever."[48]

Tax laws Church wealth, whether in the form of direct ownership of real estate and personal property or in the form of direct stocks and bonds, receives a variety of tax exemptions from local, state, and federal governments. All states exempt from real property taxation church buildings and other houses of worship and the land on which they stand. Additionally, all states exempt from taxation personal property of religious groups and property devoted to religious uses. Furthermore, the property of religious schools and colleges is exempted by all states. Also, a majority of the states exempt, in whole or in part, residences of clergymen from property taxes and exempt sales by or to churches from sales taxes. As a general rule on the state and local levels, property tax exemption requires that the property be exclusively owned by a religious body and devoted exclusively to religious purposes.

On the federal level, all religious organizations are exempt from income and gift taxes, including income from producing real property if the income is paid directly to the religious organization. At the present time, however, religious orders, as distinct from churches and associations of churches, pay a so-called unrelated business tax.[49] Thus, the Christian Brothers order pays federal taxes on the extensive income derived from its California winery.[50] Under defined conditions, the income from an unrelated business becomes subject to normal corporate and

---

[45]See D. B. Robertson, *Should Churches Be Taxed*, Westminster Press, Philadelphia, 1968, p. 60.
[46]*Church, State and Freedom*, p. 213.
[47]Martin Larson, *Church Wealth and Business Income*, Philosophical Library, New York, 1965, p. 19.
[48]Quoted in "Churches and Tax Exemption." editorial, *Journal of Church and State*, vol. 2, p. 196, Spring 1969.
[49]26 U.S.C. 510 (1950).
[50]See *De La Salle Institute v. United States*, 196 F.S. 891 (1961).

surtax rates.[51] However, in the Tax Reform Act of 1969, Congress stipulated that churches and associations of churches would become subject to the unrelated business income tax as of January 1, 1976.

Arguments for exemption   A principal argument in favor of continued tax exemption is that the exemption is really a quid pro quo. Churches, so the argument runs, provide important services to the community, such as education, charity, and caring for the ill, the homeless, and the needy. In exchange for these significant contributions, the state should give an indirect subsidy in the form of tax exemptions. A second argument maintains that churches are important instruments in the development of the community's moral fiber, in that they instill in their communicants the virtues of love of fellowmen, of charity, and of generosity toward the poor and destitute. Finally, it is argued that tax exemptions undergird the free-exercise clause. Here it is argued that, since historically and constitutionally one of the principal goals of our nation has been to provide for religious liberty, tax exemptions provide a natural method for maintaining the economic independence necessary for the exercise of religious freedom.

Arguments against exemptions   Perhaps the chief argument against exemption has already been stated: Churches are wealthy and governments need new sources of revenue to pay for the costs of increasing government services. Additionally, it is argued that there are no available data to support the proposition that churches contribute to the well-being of society or that they exercise the kind of moral influence that is beneficial to the general welfare. It is also argued that tax exemptions place a heavier burden on those who are not members of churches. Finally, it is maintained that such privileged exemptions tarnish and damage religion by, for example, inducing pastors to pursue such cultic embellishments as concrete-and-glass ego monuments.

Wisely, the Supreme Court has indicated that it will not attempt to resolve the complex problem of tax exemptions. In 1970, in a case involving church property-tax exemptions in New York, the Court upheld the exemptions as not in violation of the religion clauses of the First Amendment.[52] The majority, speaking through Chief Justice Warren E. Burger, held that there was no genuine nexus between tax exemption and establishment of religion. Such an exemption actually creates less government involvement in religion than would taxation. The majority noted that if tax exemption is a "foot in the door" leading to establishment, the second step has been long in coming.

That tax exemptions for churches and religious organizations do not violate the Constitution does not, of course, end the matter. A constitutionally permissive policy of tax exemptions does not answer the question of whether these exemptions constitute wise public policy. It may be wise for a court to avoid drafting policy here since the judicial process does not lend itself to examinations of the intricate issues involved. Nonetheless, legislative bodies should face such issues as whether,

[51]26 U.S.C. 11 (1969).
[52]*Waltz v. Tax Commission*, 90 S.Ct. 1409 (1970).

while houses of worship should be exempt, the various types of exempt church income might merit reconsideration. Exempting a house of worship from a property tax seems a natural complement to the policy implicit in the free exercise clause of the First Amendment. Exempting the income from a church-owned girdle factory is an at least questionable extension of that policy.

The churches, tax exemption, and financial disclosure Beyond the broad issues of tax exemption for churches and religious organizations is the more immediate problem of financial disclosure for religious organizations that receive federal income tax exemption. Under a provision of the Internal Revenue Code, Section 501(c)(3), the Commissioner of the Internal Revenue Service is authorized to grant income tax exemption to educational, charitable, scientific, literary, and religious nonprofit organizations *except* as to their unrelated business income. The latter clause simply means that if a religious or educational organization buys, for example, a winery, as did the Christian Brothers, the organization may continue its tax-exempt status but the status will not apply to its newly acquired unrelated business, even though the profits of the business are used to promote the educational or religious enterprise. The rationale for this is that the tax exemptions were given in order to support certain nonprofit enterprises that Congress deemed worthy of indirect encouragement, and thus a financial enterprise unrelated to the purpose of an exemption should not be covered by the congressional privilege. An organization that enjoys a Section 501 exemption might acquire unrelated businesses in a variety of ways. It might be given the business in a bequest, or, as sometimes happens, a failing or faltering business might sell out to an exempt organization on condition that the business be leased back to the original owners, thereby creating a Section 501 exemption for reasons totally unrelated to Congress's policy.

Discovering whether exempt organizations have acquired an unrelated business is not as easy as one might assume. Therefore, in 1969 Congress amended an IRS requirement on financial disclosure. Section 6033-2(g)(i) was amended to require that all Section 501 exempt organizations file annual financial disclosures *except* churches, church conventions and associations, church-related foreign missions, church-affiliated elementary and secondary schools, the exclusively religious activity of a religious order, and an *integrated auxiliary* of a church. It is the latter that has caused some concern. The IRS has defined an "integrated auxiliary" as a church-affiliated organization exempt under Section 501 whose principal activity is exclusively religious.

Thus a religious hospital or a denominational college or a church-sponsored retirement home would not be considered an integrated auxiliary since its principal activities are not exclusively religious. Such institutions would be required, then, to file annual financial disclosures. The net result is that fewer tax-exempt organizations, including religious organizations, are excused from filing annual financial disclosures. However, while this was probably the intent of Congress, it does raise a question about the role of the IRS in defining a church. Many so-called hierarchical churches, such as the Mormon and Catholic churches, do not give separate legal identity to all components of the church, whereas many congregational churches, such as the Baptist, operate as autonomous units and not as part of a greater church organization. In effect, the integrated-auxiliary exemption favors the hierarchical churches. Some hold that this unwisely, even unconstitutionally, intrudes into the internal life of churches.[53] They would contend that such a government regulation has the effect of defining the mission of churches and thus chills the right of free exercise of religion. What seems to be lost in the argument is the fact that Congress is extending a privilege when it extends tax exemptions. A degree of government monitoring is probably required here in order to ensure that congressional intent is not subverted. Unless one argues that Congress could never tax a religious organization, whatever the nature of its principal activity, then some government involvement in the internal life of an exempt organization is the price of the exemption. So long as the government grants tax exemptions to churches, there is necessarily a definitional problem. Churches may continue to define their religious missions, but the government must establish and define the limits of its own policy, otherwise any group or person would be entitled to the exemption by merely advancing the claim.

CONCLUSION

The twentieth century has witnessed an extensive campaign to eliminate sectarianism in state action. In part, this is due to the growing numbers of Jews and nonbelievers who, for different reasons, find it offensive for the state to foster or participate in religious life. Furthermore, the tendency of Protestantism to multiply into sects has strengthened the argument that in a religiously plural society it is impractical for the state to play an active role in the religious life of the community. However, in pressing a neo-Jeffersonian position, the advocates of separation have tended to demand that the wall of separation be raised to absolute heights. Such a position ignores the fact that "no establishment" and religious liberty should be complementary, not contradictory, rights.[54] Separation was intended to serve religious liberty, not to do it a disservice. Freedom of religion and separation are a continuum; if either is pressed too far the other will suffer. As Justice Powell observed, "this Nation's history has not been one of entirely sanitized separation between Church and State."[55] Unquestionably, church-state issues are potentially divisive, but that begins, rather than ends, the constitutional inquiry. To act otherwise would confer on the no-establishment clause an absolute quality supported neither by our history nor by the pragmatism so essential to policy formulation in this area.

[53]See John Baker, ed., *Taxation and the Free Exercise Clause*, Baptist Joint Committee on Public Affairs, Washington, D.C., 1978
[54]For a forceful presentation of this view, see Madalyn Murray O'Hair, *Freedom under Siege*, J. P. Tarcher, Los Angeles, 1974.
[55]*Committee for Public Education v. Nyquist*, 93 S.Ct. 2959 (1973).

UNUSUAL RELIGIOUS NEEDS

The First Amendment's ban on governmental laws that prohibit the free exercise of religion is not an item that looms large in the minds of religious Americans. Most Americans worship and practice their religion as they choose without pausing to consider the issue of legal impediments to religious freedom. The reason for this is quite obviously that the dominant religions in America do not require their adherents to act or refrain from acting in ways contrary to the law. Catholics, Methodists, Baptists, and Lutherans, for example, may conduct their worship services and their daily lives in accordance with the requirements and tenets of their religious beliefs with little or no thought about conflicts with state laws. Yet for thousands of Americans the free-exercise clause does not always assure them that they will be allowed either to worship or conduct their lives in accordance with their religious convictions. The problem normally is not that the government directly attempts through legislation to proscribe or prescribe religious conduct. The problems that arise are usually the indirect consequence of the normal operation of the civil and criminal laws. Thus in the 1878 case of *Reynolds v. United States*, Reynolds, a Mormon living in the territory of Utah, was convicted under a federal bigamy statute for having more than one wife.[56] At that time the teachings of the Latter-Day Saints generally required male members to practice polygamy on penalty of damnation. The trial court rejected Reynold's defense of a religious duty to practice polygamy. In upholding his conviction the Supreme Court made the following observations:

> Laws are made for the government of actions, and while they cannot interfere with mere religious belief and opinions, they may with practices. Suppose one believed that human sacrifices were a necessary part of religious worship, would it be seriously contended that the civil government under which he lived could not interfere to prevent a sacrifice? Or if a wife religiously believed it was her duty to burn herself upon the funeral pile of her dead husband, would it be beyond the power of the civil government to prevent her carrying her belief into practice? . . . To permit this would be to make the professed doctrines of religious belief superior to the law of the land, and in effect to permit every citizen to become a law unto himself. Government could exist only in name under such circumstances.[57]

The *Reynolds* decision makes what would appear to be an entirely reasonable assertion, that is, that we are not always free to act on our beliefs. It would be unreasonable to expect that individuals could immunize their conduct in the name of free exercise of religion. On the other hand, the *Reynolds* decision ought not to be interpreted to imply that conduct can never be protected in the name of free exercise of religion. Surely the free-exercise clause is intended to do more than simply protect passive meditation on religious beliefs. To exercise a religion freely implies some degree of free conduct. When religious conduct collides with

[56]98 U.S. 145.
[57]Ibid., pp. 166–167.

the state, it may be necessary to balance the needs of the state and the religious needs of the individual. The balancing may occur when the state priority is first established, as in the case of colonial adjustments to Quaker needs, such as allowing Quakers to affirm an oath rather than swear to an oath. Administrative adjustment of state laws to religious needs is probably more common than an initial legislative adjustment, but an example of the latter can be seen in the military draft exemptions for members of historic peace churches, dating back to 1864.[58] Whether these adjustments are simply a matter of state grace or are constitutionally required is probably of less importance than the recognition that a degree of state accommodation to religious needs has been a part of American history. Nonetheless, formulating a clear statement of the constitutional law of the free-exercise clause cannot be attempted here. However, some insights can be gained by examining cases in which claims of religious exemption were raised as a defense against the application of otherwise valid state laws.

EXEMPTING RELIGIOUS CONDUCT: A THREE-FOLD TEST

The Mormon polygamy cases, which stretch from the 1870s through the 1940s, offer little in the way of a direct help in formulating constitutional policy in this area.[59] The cases, however, do suggest that religious practices, however sincerely held and central to one's faith, that are contrary to civil or criminal laws will receive no accommodation under the free-exercise clause if accommodation would defeat the purpose of the law. Thus lurking in the background of the polygamy cases are some hints as to the outer limits of constitutional policy. In situations of unusual religious practices or unique religious needs, several avenues need to be explored. One is the fact of infringement; that is, does the application of the law in fact infringe on a core or central element of a religious faith, or merely work an inconvenience on the faith? in the 1870s, there was little doubt that polygamy was a core element of Mormon faith and that the application of a bigamy law defeated this central element of the Mormon faith. On the other hand, there are religious practices that are less central to one's faith, and in such instances the application of state proscriptions or limitations would not defeat religious exercise. For example, prayer is an important part of many faiths, but most Christian faiths do not require a fixed and regularized practice of prayer. However, the Islamic faith requires ritual prayer five times daily. Thus, would a Muslim prisoner be entitled to ritual prayer even in the face of conflicting prison regulations?

This brings us to the second part of the policy, that is, the sincerity or good faith of a claimed exemption. Perhaps nothing can make constitutional policy in this area look more ridiculous than bogus and insincere claims for a particular religious exercise. In the Mormon cases

[58]For the contemporary period, see *Gillette v. United States*, 401 U.S. 437 (1971), and *Wilson v. United States*, 398 U.S. 333 (1970).
[59]See *Reynolds* case and *Davis v. Blason*, 133 U.S. 333 (1890), and *Cleveland v. United States*, 329 U.S. 14 (1946).

there was little to suggest that the religious claims were pretexts intended to cloak debauchery. The claims of Reynolds were undoubtedly bona fide. On the other hand, the good faith of some claimants in recent drug cases might be questioned. In a 1968 case a defendant was charged with violating federal laws governing the use of marijuana and LSD.[60] The defendant claimed to be a minister in the Neo-American Church. The church was headed by a Chief Boo-Hoo, and the defendant was a primate, or area supervisor, of the Boo-Hoos. The church subscribed to the following principles:

Everyone has the right to expand his consciousness and stimulated visionary experience by whatever means he considers desirable and proper with interference from anyone; . . . The psychedelic substances, such as LSD, are the true Host of the Church, not drugs. They are sacramental foods, manifestations of the Grace of God, of the infinite imagination of the Self, and therefore belong to everyone.[61]

The Church symbol was the three-eyed toad; its official song, "Puff, The Magic Dragon," and its motto, "Victory Over Horseshit."[62] Finally, the neo-American Church lacked a formal theology and a belief in a supreme being.

The facts of this 1968 case suggest that the claims for religious exemption were transparently bogus. As the federal court concluded, "It is clear that the desire to use drugs and to enjoy drugs for their own sake, regardless of religious experience, is the coagulant of this organization, and the reason for its existence."[63] Indeed, the facts of the case raise a substantial question not only about the good faith of the claim but additionally about the legitimacy of the Neo-American Church as a religious as distinct from a recreational organization. Freedom of religious exercise is not a license for flimflam.

In other contexts, however, the delicate task of inquiring into the sincerity of a religious claim is far from easy and poses substantial problems for the judiciary. Although the Supreme Court has never indicated directly that such inquiries are permissible, it has, at least on one occasion, avoided striking down such an inquiry.[64] Some lower courts have taken this as an implicit endorsement. Thus in the California peyote case the Supreme Court of California ruled that a member of the Native American Church, a religious organization of Indians, could not be convicted for violating a law prohibiting the unauthorized possession of peyote, a hallucinogen. The California court concluded that peyote played a central role as a sacramental symbol in the religion of the Native American Church and that the religious claim was honest and made in good faith.[65]

[60]*United States v. Kuch*, 288 F. Supp. 439.

[61]Ibid., p. 443.

[62]Ibid., p. 444.

[63]Ibid.

[64]See *United States v. Ballard*, 322 U.S. 78 (1944).

[65]*Califorai v. Woody*, 394 p. 2d 813 (1964); cf. *North Carolina v. Bullard*, 148 S.E. 2d 565 (1966).

There are obvious pitfalls in such inquiries. Clearly it would not be appropriate for courts to inquire into the truth or falsity or reasonableness of religious claims. People must be free to believe what they choose to believe without fear that the government will challenge the accuracy of their beliefs.[66] Good faith, then, should never depend on the truth of a claim, but rather on the sincerity of one espousing a religious belief. Even such a limited inquiry into the bona fides of a claim is a delicate task. For example, would the sincerity of a religious claim have to be rejected if in fact the claimant entertained doubts as to the accuracy of an espoused religious claim? This could be a critical issue in prosecutions for fraud where the defendant obtained money or property in the name of a religious organization, and claimed that solicitation for a religious cause was a tenet of his religion.

Yet the honesty and sincerity of a religious claim does not end in the inquiry. Before a religious claim of exemption can be granted, not only must there be proof of an actual infringement and proof of the honesty of the claim, it must also be established that an exemption or accommodation will not defeat the valid purpose of the law in question. In other words, could religious exemption be granted and the purpose of the particular law still be accomplished? Thus in the polygamy cases, could the purposes sought to be achieved by a proscription against bigamy be accomplished if sincere religious polygamists were given exemptions? Does a bigamy law have to be strictly and uniformly applied in order to accomplish the state's policy? Certainly there are laws which would seem to demand a uniform and strict application, with no possibility of accommodation or exemption. Proscriptions against murder would hardly allow exemptions for religiously motivated infanticide. And in *McGowan v. Maryland* the Supreme Court ruled that in order to accomplish a uniform day of rest, the state could establish a Sunday closing law and was not required to grant exemptions to those who observed the Sabbath on another day.[67] In answer to the argument that there were alternatives to a Sunday closing law, the Court noted:

> . . . the State's purpose is not merely to provide a one-day-in-seven work stoppage. In addition to this, the State seeks to set one day apart from all others as a day of rest, repose, recreation and tranquility—a day which all members of the family and community have the opportunity to spend and enjoy together, a day on which there exists relative quiet and dissassociation from the everyday intensity of commercial activities, a day on which people may visit friends and relatives who are not available during working days.[68]

However, in a 1963 case the Court reached a contrary conclusion in a South Carolina unemployment compensation case. Adell Sherbert, a Seventh-Day Adventist, was discharged by her employer because she would not work on Saturday. She subsequently refused to accept suitable and available employment for the same reason, that is, that her

[66]See *United States v. Ballard*, 322 U.S. 78 (1944).
[67]366 U.S. 420 (1961).
[68]Ibid., p. 450.

religious precepts precluded Saturday work. Under the state law she was disqualified from unemployment benefits for refusing available and suitable work.[69] The Court concluded that the statute did work an infringement on Sherbert's free exercise by forcing her to choose between her religious precepts and unemployment benefits. Given the substantial infringement involved, the Court concluded that only a compelling state interest could justify uniform application of the law. The Court rejected abstract state fears of possible abuses if exemptions were allowed, noting that it was the responsibility of the state to demonstrate that such abuses could not be regulated. In short, granting a religious exemption for those who observe a Sabbath other than Sunday would not render the statute unworkable.[70]

A similar process of balancing occurred in *Wisconsin v. Yoder*.[71] Yoder was a member of the Old Order of Amish and refused, on religious grounds, to send his children to school beyond the eighth grade. Since the children involved were under age sixteen, Yoder's action placed him in violation of the state's compulsory school-attendance law. The Court reasoned that in order for the state to prevail against a legitimate religious claim, it would be necessary to establish either (1) that the state requirement did not deny the free exercise of a religious belief, or (2) that the state had an interest of sufficient magnitude to override the claimed religious interest of Yoder. After examining the Amish religion the Court concluded that:

> The Amish in this case have convincingly demonstrated the sincerity of their religious beliefs, the interrelationship of belief with their mode of life, the vital role which belief and daily conduct play in the continued survival of Old Order Amish communities and their religious organization, and the hazards presented by the State's enforcement of a statute generally valid as to others. Beyond this, they have carried the even more difficult burden of demonstrating the adequacy of their alternative mode of continuing informal vocational education in terms of precisely those overall interests that the State advances in support of its program of compulsory high school education.[72]

CONCLUSION

It seems axiomatic that at times religious conduct must yield to important state interests. Freedom of religious exercise cannot operate as an absolute bar to the normal operation of a state's laws and administrative regulations. Yet even if the state may choose to label religious conduct unlawful, that does not create any irrebuttable argument. Free religious exercise necessarily implies a degree of protected religious conduct, and therefore claimants must be afforded an opportunity to

[69]*Sherbert v. Verner*, 374 U.S. 398 (1963).
[70]Indeed the law already granted exemption for those conscientiously opposed to Sunday work, ibid., p. 406.
[71]406 U.S. 205 (1972).
[72]Ibid., p. 235.

set forth arguments for exemption. The tests have been judicially devised for determining when valid state laws must yield to religious conduct are far from satisfactory, particularly to the extent that they interject the judiciary into the delicate areas of religious sincerity and religious legitimacy. Drawing lines in sensitive and complicated areas will rarely produce results acceptable to all, yet the presence of pitfalls is not an excuse for failing to adjust our laws to the sometimes unique and unusual needs of religious sects. The fact that bogus claims sometimes make religious conduct seem like a joke is not a sufficient reason for judicial withdrawal from this area. The problems will not go away. The increase of religious pluralism in the United States in the past quarter of a century has brought with it a number of new religions with requirements and needs not represented by mainline Christian and Jewish sects; this factor alone suggests that the judiciary will face increasing demands for accommodation and adjustment. The threefold test of degree of infringement, good faith, and government interest provides at least a beginning point in balancing societal needs and free religious exercise.

5 CRIMINAL JUSTICE

The issue of crime in America is perennial. Every year the FBI publishes its Uniform Crime Reports, and every year the public becomes alarmed at the ever-increasing rate of crimes against persons and property. The alarm is not entirely misplaced. While many crimes go unreported, particularly burglary and larceny,[1] the amount of reported crime is extensive. As suggested by the accompanying illustration, crime is a relatively common occurrence in the United States. While this "crime clock" inaccurately suggests that there is a precise timetable for the occurrence of certain crimes, it is a fair and graphic way of conveying the scope of the problem.[2]

Clearly a reported level of approximately 11 million serious crimes a year cannot be lightly dismissed. Nor can the rate of increase be ignored. Although it is doubtful whether we could agree on what rate of crime is "acceptable," still there is a level beyond which we cannot go, a level beyond which individuals cease to enjoy the kind of environment thought to be necessary for human growth and development. An environment that threatens us with murder, assault, robbery, rape, burglary, and larceny is hardly one that enables the human personality to develop to its full potential. Such an environment may indeed already have been reached in certain neighborhoods, particularly minority neighborhoods, in some of our large central cities. Here the trustworthiness and stability of the social order may indeed be imperiled.[3] Yet, as alarming as the situation may be in some areas, one needs to approach the issue with a certain amount of caution and even skepticism.

Crime statistics are not only unreliable, but further, in the hands of some individuals they are manipulated, exaggerated, and oversimplified. The "crime clocks" seem calculated to strike terror in the hearts of all Americans and thereby to undermine trust in the social order. And in the hands of certain politicians the slippery crime statistics become an agenda for attacks on the courts and on parts of the Bill of Rights.[4]

[1]See Phillip Ennis, *Criminal Victimization in the United States*, National Opinion Research Center, 1967.

[2]The table is based on aggregate data and is only intended to suggest that offenses occur frequently rather than to give the precise regularity of certain offenses.

[3]See President's Commission on Law Enforcement and the Administration of Justice, *The Challenge of Crime in a Free Society*, 1967, pp. 35–37.

[4]See Hugh D. Graham and Ted R. Gurr, *The History of Violence in America*, Bantam Books, New York, 1969, chap. 13.

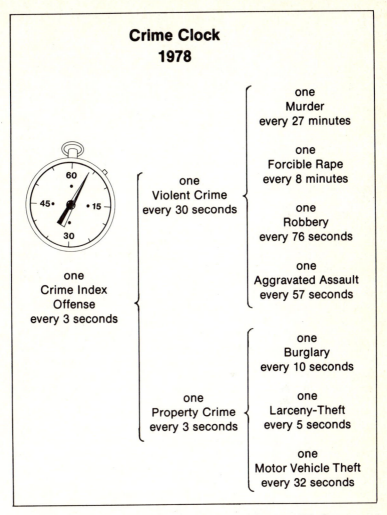

Crime Clock
1978

one
Violent Crime
every 30 seconds

one
Murder
every 27 minutes

one
Forcible Rape
every 8 minutes

one
Robbery
every 76 seconds

one
Aggravated Assault
every 57 seconds

one
Crime Index
Offense
every 3 seconds

one
Property Crime
every 3 seconds

one
Burglary
every 10 seconds

one
Larceny-Theft
every 5 seconds

one
Motor Vehicle Theft
every 32 seconds

Source: *Uniform Crime Reports for the United States, 1979*, Government Printing Office, Washington, D.C., 1979, p. ix.

Loose talk about waging a war on crime and about law and order must be viewed with some concern and caution for at least two reasons. First, the war on crime has proven to be extremely costly in terms of dollars and singularly unsuccessful, at least insofar as the crime rate is concerned. Second, such talk tends to oversimplify or even ignore the proper role of the criminal law in a free society. Safety is not the ultimate goal of the criminal law but rather a byproduct. The ultimate goal of the criminal law is to produce an environment which enhances the capacity for individual growth and development. As the late Herbert Packer stated, "The prevention of crime is an essential aspect of the environmental protection required if autonomy is to flourish. It is, however, a negative aspect and one which, pursued with single-minded zeal, may end up creating an environment in which all are safe but none is free."[5]

The coercive elements of the criminal law—the array of punishments and the likelihood of public humiliation and disgrace—add an element of high risk to this particular kind of social control. The risk of a negative relationship between human freedom and the criminal law is one of the reasons why democratic societies saddle the substantive criminal law with a host of procedural restraints. Our close attention to the process, due to those caught up in the machinery of the criminal system, is a reflection of our collective judgment and fear that today's right result without due process will be turned on us tomorrow for the wrong results.

THE QUEST FOR CRIMINAL JUSTICE

While in the broad sense the ultimate goal of the criminal law is the enhancement of individual freedom, justice is the narrow goal to which the system is committed. As St. Augustine observed, "Set justice aside, then, and what are kingdoms but great robberies?" Legal justice in the criminal system begins with the definition of crimes—the authoritative process of declaring what conduct merits the criminal label. Not only must the process be authoritative, but the conduct labled criminal should be limited by two factors. The conduct to be deterred should be clearly and significantly harmful to persons or property, not condoned by any substantial portion of the society, and the label should be used only when there are no appropriate alternatives to the criminal sanction.

Fair and equal justice   But justice here does not end with the definition of a crime. Justice also concerns itself with the administration of the criminal sanctions. The just criminal law is one that is administered fairly and equally by the police, the prosecutors, the courts, and the penal institutions. There is no litmus-paper test for determining equal and fair treatment. However, there are a number of statutory and/or constitutional provisions prevailing in most jurisdictions that establish procedural safeguards. These procedural safeguards are largely intended to ensure fair and equal treatment of the formally accused; hence, the bulk of the following rights are intended to ensure a fair trial rather than fair and equal treatment by the police and the prosecutor:

Limits on the Conduct of the Police and Prosecutor

1 No unreasonable searches and seizures

2 No arrests except on probable cause

3 No coerced confessions or illegal interrogation

4 No entrapment, i.e., no official inducement to commit a previously uncontemplated crime

[5]Herbert L. Packer, *The Limits of the Criminal Sanction*, Stanford University Press, Stanford, Calif., 1968, p. 65.

Defendant's Pretrial Rights
1 to the writ of habeas corpus
2 to prompt arraignment
3 upon arrest, to secure legal counsel and/or contact a close friend or relative
4 to no excessive bail
5 to be informed of the charges against him
Defendant's Trial Rights
1 to a speedy and public trial before an impartial judge and jury and in a court of competent jurisdiction
2 to a jury selected from a representative cross-section of the community
3 to a trial in a judicial atmosphere free of prejudice, fear, and outside interference
4 to compulsory process
5 to confront all witnesses
6 to no compulsory self-incrimination
7 to adequate counsel for defense
8 to no cruel or unusual punishment
9 to appeal convictions
10 to no double jeopardy

Why do democratic societies place such emphasis on justice in the criminal process? At times the emphasis would seem lopsided. Why should we extend so many rights to kidnappers, vicious murderers, and armed robbers? The pain of the victims and the anguish of their loved ones seem almost unnoticed. The answer is at once simple and complex. When the state, with its monopoly on murder, focuses its coercive machinery on an individual, we want to ensure that the innocent are protected as well as that the guilty are punished. If a society accepts the dignity of all men and the worth and value of all human life, then such a society cannot easily or cavalierly risk the life or dignity of one man. When such a society proceeds with caution against alleged criminals, when it establishes and conforms to procedural safeguards protecting the rights of defendants in the criminal process, then such a society has made a vast stride toward achieving criminal justice.

DUE PROCESS: A MODEL

The constitutional requirements of due process in the various stages of the criminal process do not necessarily comport with reality. Criminal justice, as practiced, is far less attentive to the constitutionality of extant procedures than one might infer from a simple reading of a defendant's pretrial and trial rights. The need for efficient measures in handling a large workload with limited resources often appears to dictate that the operative model of criminal justice take shortcuts. Quite independent of workload considerations the administrative model of criminal justice has a natural bias against the requirements of due process. Due process begins with the assumption of legal innocence and the consequent need for the state to prove, theoretically at trial, the guilt of a defendant. On the other hand the administrative model proceeds from a different assumption. At an early stage in the administration of justice the police and/or the district attorney's office make a decision about the guilt or innocence of a prospective defendant. This administrative screening process tends to eliminate those who are innocent in fact or guilty in fact but innocent in law, that is, those for whom the state would be unable to prove legal guilt. Thus the police, after further investigation, may release someone they arrested either because a witness refuses to cooperate or because they become convinced that the person arrested did not commit the offense. Or if charges are filed by the police a prosecutor may decide not to proceed for any number of reasons, including lack of sufficient legal evidence or because the prosecutor is convinced that the accused is innocent.

One result of this filtering process is to convince the personnel in the various criminal-justice units that those individuals who are not screened out are factually guilty. Thus there is a tension between this administrative conclusion about the probable guilt of a defendant and the legal presumption that the defendant is innocent. This legal presumption dictates that the state proceed against the individual by well-defined procedures and requirements, such as the requirement that seizures of evidence be based on probable cause, and such rights as arraignment, bail, preliminary hearing, and indictment. For those who are convinced that a defendant is in fact guilty, the requirements of due process may appear at times to be unnecessary and undesirable roadblocks to justice. The solicitude that the Constitution accords to probable transgressors of the criminal law may turn some actors in the criminal-justice system into cynics who are willing to quietly ignore the Constitution in order to apprehend and punish the guilty.

An unchecked desire to punish the guilty, however, can become a corrosive force. Somewhere in our society there must be an institutional force that restrains police/prosecutor impulses to push law enforcement to the outer limits. Our constitutional system establishes a balanced set of priorities. Power is given to the government to govern— for example, power to protect society from criminals—but the Constitution evidences a certain distrust of unchecked power. Indeed the Fourth, Fifth, Sixth, and Eighth Amendments check the power of judges, police, and prosecutors. In short, under our constitutional system we are to be neither totally safe nor totally free. This message requires constant reiteration or it will be lost. Law enforcement must never be allowed to operate in a culture in which legalisms, that is, procedural due process, have become so denigrated that they no longer serve to restrain the exercise of power.

One method for reinforcing the legal culture in which the criminal justice system operates is for the appellate judiciary to review and examine elements of the system. We turn to the judiciary not because it is necessarily the most effective body to supervise the system but simply because it is often the only governmental body that is willing to examine police, prosecutor, trial court, and prison practices. The criminal justice agencies, especially those involved at the pretrial stage, that is, the police and prosecutors, have been historically among the least supervised agencies in government. For a variety of reasons, some quite sound, police and prosecutors have been accorded wide discretion to chart their own courses. Those agencies of local government most directly accountable to the public—city councils, mayors, and county governing boards—have traditionally steered a wide path around the internal affairs of law-enforcement agencies. Indeed, in some sense Americans have come to accept and even demand that the politically responsible agencies of government stay out of law enforcement. In view of the minimal amount of supervison given to criminal justice agencies there is a need for some institution in the government to set constitutional standards for these agencies. Partly by default, then, the task has become the responsibility of the judiciary and especially the responsibility of the Supreme Court.

THE SUPREME COURT AND CRIMINAL JUSTICE

The judiciary has assumed a major role in setting standards for criminal justice agencies not merely by default of the other branches of government; courts have a role in this area also because of their knowledge and their independence. The judiciary, as a part of the criminal justice network, has not been particularly reluctant to set constitutional standards for those aspects of criminal justice that come within the immediate competence and special preview of judges, such as trial procedures. The judiciary has, however, been less willing to set standards for police and prosecutors and for correctional agencies, the pre- and post-trial parts of the system. Clearly judges do not possess the same degree of professional competence in these areas as they do in matters of criminal litigation. Neither by training nor by physical proximity to the other components of the system could judges claim to be professionally qualified in law enforcement and corrections. Yet the judiciary probably has as much if not more insight into these areas than currently obtains in many legislative bodies. Beyond whatever competence the judiciary may possess in matters of criminal justice, the judiciary has another advantage, namely its independence. At the federal level and in many states judges have, in effect, life tenure, and this independence allows the judiciary to assume some risks that actors in the other branches of government are often politically unable to assume. Setting constitutional standards is often risky, at least to the extent that it gives the *appearance* of coddling criminals. Yet somewhere in our system of government the principles of the Fourth, Fifth, Sixth, and Eighth Amendments must be kept alive. Ensuring that the principles of these amendments remain alive and vital in a changing environment is a matter of prudence. The wide discretion exercised by police, prosecutors, and correction agencies must, on occasion, be checked against the priorities set forth in the Bill of Rights. Defining procedural due process, that is, fairness, is a duty that courts can and should discharge.

We need to recognize, however, that courts, including the Supreme Court, are not especially powerful in our system of government. The judicial process has neither the power of the sword nor the power of the purse, only the power of words. The judicial process is inherently limited. It has no self-starter, no administrative resources, and, indeed, no constitutional power, to monitor the norm. Failure to accept a new norm cannot be sanctioned directly. Beyond persuasion, the judiciary must resort to indirect sanctions, such as exclusionary rules. These rules exclude evidence taken in violation of a norm, for example, confessions obtained by violence or threats. Exclusionary rules do not, of course, directly control the daily behavior of participants in the criminal process. Such rules merely attempt to deny to the prosecutor any benefit obtained by violating a norm. The sanction is thus limited to those situations in which the prosecutor decides to accuse the aggrieved individual and to take advantage of any benefit derived from violating the norm, such as introducing a coerced confession or illegally seized evidence.

Supreme Court sanctions are of limited utility in regulating the system of criminal justice not only because of the limited power of the judiciary but also because of the nature of our federal system.[6] The system of criminal justice is largely a responsibility of the states, and the federal judiciary has only limited power to intrude into a state's criminal system. Federalism is, thus, a potent force in the criminal law. The states have the primary responsibility for maintaining order on a daily basis and under this system they are at liberty to develop their own criminal procedures and have done so. Our constitutional system of reserved powers for the states, while greatly altered in the past seventy-five years, still presupposes that the states have inherent powers. But the same Constitution that outlines a federal system also contains an amendment, the Fourteenth, which was probably intended to weaken the system of reserved powers.

The Fourteenth Amendment, adopted in 1868 as a Civil War amendment, stipulates that no state shall deny to any person life, liberty, or property without due process of law and that no state shall deny to any person the equal protection of the laws. In the aftermath of the Civil War, the Supreme Court all but forgot about these clauses. It refused to tax federal-state relations by interpreting them in such a way as to irritate the already strained relations between the central government and the states.[7]

For nearly sixty years after the adoption of the Fourteenth Amendment, the court cast a suspicious eye on claims of denials of due process and equal protection of the laws in state criminal cases. During those sixty years the Court seldom reviewed a state criminal case, and when it did the review was pro forma.[8]

Gradually the Court reexamined its earlier position. Undoubtedly, this reexamination was due in part to the failure of many of the states to develop adequate procedures to ensure that reason and not prejudice and passion guided the courts and law-enforcement agencies in criminal cases. Since the early 1930s, the court has become an active

---

[6]For an examination of the impact of or compliance with Supreme Court decisions in the area of criminal justice, see Stephen L. Wasby, *The Impact of the United States Supreme Court*, Dorsey Press, Homewood, Ill., 1970, pp. 147–169.

[7]See *Hurtado v. California*, 110 U.S. 516 (1884); cf. *Moore v. Dempsey*, 261 U.S. 84 (1923).

[8]For example, *Frank v. Mangum*, 237 U.S. 309, 326 (1915).

force in state criminal justice. The court has intruded in the areas of arrest, search, and seizure, in the matter of coerced confessions, in jury selection, in counsel for defense. Until recently, the Court has been hesitant to impose on the states the same procedural restrictions that are imposed on federal law-enforcement agencies and federal courts.

Beginning in the 1930s, the court attempted to get the states to follow the principle of "fair trial."[9] As used by the court, fair trial was a concept of minimal justice. When the Court was confronted with a set of facts alleging a denial of criminal due process by a state, it asked whether the alleged violation was one of those "fundamental principles of liberty and justice which be at the base of all our civil and political institutions."[10] Under this approach to due process, the Court becomes endowed with the power periodically to examine state procedures to see if they conform to what the Court considers at a given time to be the "fundamental principles of liberty and justice." Thus, the due process clause became the conscience clause of the Constitution, and the Court acted as the guardian of this conscience.

Criminal justice and the Warren and Burger courts   The minimal justice or "fair trial" approach of the *Palko* case was abandoned in the early 1960s. Instead, the Warren Court opted for "nationalizing" the major procedural rights of the Fourth, Fifth, and Sixth Amendments. Formerly, these rights applied only to federal criminal cases. Under the nationalizing approach, the Court incorporated many of these rights into the due process clause of the Fourteenth Amendment, thereby making them applicable to state criminal cases.[11]

It is not likely that these constitutional changes will be reversed by the Burger Court. Direct reversal of such recent decisions would undermine the integrity of the judiciary. On the other hand, the new majority is less inclined to continue the process of incorporation and more inclined to limit the scope of earlier decisions.[12] Close attention to procedural due process, a hallmark of the Warren majority, has been replaced, in some degree, by more attention to the demands of police and prosecutors for wider procedural latitude in enforcing the criminal laws.[13] The skepticism about law enforcement implicit in many of the Warren Court decisions has been replaced by a greater willingness to temper procedural restraints, presumably in order to allow the criminal justice system to cope with the need for speed and efficiency in what many believe is an overburdened system.

[9]*Palko v. Connecticut*, 302 U.S. 319 (1937).

[10]Herbert v. Louisiana, 272 U.S. 312 (1926).

[11]See *Mapp v. Ohio*, 367 U.S. 643 (1961), illegal searches and seizures; *Gideon v. Wainwright*, 372 U.S. 335 (1963), counsel for defense; *Malloy v. Hogan*, 378 U.S. 1 (1964), no compulsory self-incrimination; *Pointer v. Texas*, 380 U.S. 400 (1965), confrontation of witnesses; *Parker v. Gladden*, 385 U.S. 363 (1966), trial by impartial jury; *Klopfer v. North Carolina*, 386 U.S. 21 (1967), speedy trial; *Washington v. Texas*, 388 U.S. 14 (1967), compulsory process; *Benton v. Maryland*, 395 U.S. 784 (1969), double jeopardy.

[12]See *Harris v. New York*, 401 U.S. 222 (1971).

[13]See for example, *Kirby v. Illinois*, 406 U.S. 682 (1972) limiting; *United States v. Wade*, 388 U.S. 218 (1967), regarding right to counsel at a police lineup.

This heightened concern for efficiency and ease in law enforcement may be a judicial reaction to the "law and order" issue of the late 1960s. Whatever the reason for the shift in policy emphasis, it does reveal a fundamental misconception of the issue of crime control. The answers to an overburdened system are not likely to be found in the judiciary. The judiciary did not create the problem, and it cannot solve it. If answers are to be found, they surely must come from legislative bodies and from the city managers, mayors, and governors.

There is a more troubling issue that arises out of the shift in Supreme Court policy. The shift is a marked departure from the fundamental responsibility of the judiciary in the rule of law, to the principle of legality. The police-prosecutor bureaucracy operates largely in a setting of secrecy and informality. Discretion is enormous, public accountability minimal, and oversight by legislative bodies or by outside executive officers limited. In consequence, there is a temptation, in an atmosphere of secrecy, to operate with ease and informality. Yet ease and informality, particularly given the pressures on the system, breed arbitrary and capricious conduct, and it is to this issue that the principle of legality is directed. Legality abhors a vacuum, eschews ease and informality, and instead demands procedural regularity and fairness. The principle commands that a "legal standard be applied to the individual with scrupulous fairness in order to minimize the chances of convicting the innocent, protect against abuse of official power, and generate an atmosphere of impartial justice."[14]

The halt in the revolution in criminal justice is by no means evident in all areas of the criminal process. For example, the Burger Court frequently struck a balance that is basically favorable to the defendant's trial rights.[15] Yet, while the trial stage is of great indirect importance to the criminal process, it is, perhaps, less important than the pretrial stage. The pretrial stage is dispositive of the vast bulk of criminal cases. A relatively small percentage of criminal cases actually go to trial; most cases are either disposed of by a negotiated plea or are dismissed. Furthermore, the trial stage is by far the most open stage, long subject to public view and strongly attached to a system of accountability and review.

The above is not intended to imply that there is no need for further extension of the principle of legality at the trial stage, but rather to suggest that a more critical issue is the reduction of arbitrariness in the pretrial stage; yet it is this area where the Burger Court appears to be least sensitive to the principle of legality. The evidence to support this is especially strong in the areas of arrest, search, and interrogation.

"FOR A MAN'S HOME IS HIS CASTLE"

The history of American liberty is full of little paradoxes. One of the more instructive paradoxes in the development of the right against unreason-

---

[14]Sanford Kadish, "Legal Norm and Discretion in Police and Sentencing Processes." Harvard Law Review, vol. 75, p. 904, 1962.

[15]See *Argersinger v. Hamlin*, 92 S.Ct. 2006 (1972), right of trial counsel extended; *Strunk v. United States*, 93 S.Ct. 2260 (1973), right to a speedy trial reinforced.

able searches and seizures concerns a great eighteenth-century empire-builder and defender of liberty, William Pitt, Earl of Chatham. One of the most notable defenses of the sanctity of the home was made by Pitt: "The poorest man may in his cottage bid defiance to all the forces of the Crown. It may be frail, its roof may shake; the wind may blow through it; the storms may enter,—the rain may enter—but the King of England cannot enter."

At the time of the famous John Wilkes case in the early 1760s, it was Pitt who led the opposition against the use of general warrants—warrants that were issued by the executive and that did not specify either the person or persons to be arrested or the places to be searched or the things to be seized.

Americans have a special fondness for this eighteenth-century giant. Pitt was one of the few true friends of the American colonists in the British government. When the colonists objected to the Stamp Act, it was Pitt who said: "I rejoice that America has resisted. Three millions of people, so dead to all the feelings of liberty, as voluntarily to submit to be slaves, would have been fit instruments to make slaves of the rest." But Pitt, advocate of the American cause, foe of despotic government, was also a man who engaged in a long war with France to build the British Empire. Thus Pitt issued three general warrants in 1760 to apprehend French spies. In the same year, Pitt, ironically, precipitated the colonial battle over writs of assistance. In 1760, as principal minister of the Crown, he issued instruction to the colonial governors to prevent American trade with the French and to diligently enforce the acts of trade. The era of salutary neglect came to an end. But enforcement in face of the colonial smuggling trade meant the use of writs of assistance, writs similar in all respects to general warrants.

In looking back over the career of William Pitt, one might conclude that unrestricted power is safe in the hands of a man like Pitt, a man with a deep commitment to freedom, a man who strayed from the path of liberty only temporarily and then in the interests of a nation at war. It is easy to close one's eyes to the use of arbitrary powers to catch spies. But it was Pitt himself, in a sequel to the battle against general warrants, who said, "Unlimited power is apt to corrupt the minds of those who possess it." Free men cannot gamble their liberties on the chance that the powerful machinery of the state will always be in the hands of a William Pitt. Pitt's ministry was followed by those of John Stuart, Earl of Bute, and George Grenville. It was during the ministry of the narrow-minded and autocratic Grenville that general warrants were issued against John Wilkes for printing criticisms of King George III, and it was also during his ministry that the hated Stamp Act was introduced in the Colonies.

The fourth amendment: a second-class right?   Democracies must assume that they will have the well-intentioned, able, but autocratic Grenvilles with them. Thus, as the late Jerome Frank stated, "A sane, decent, civilized society must provide some oasis, some shelter from public scrutiny, some insulated enclosure, some enclave, some inviolate place which is a man's castle."[16] The Bill of Rights does attempt to provide some measure of protection of privacy. The Fourth Amendment reads:

> The right of the people to be secure in their persons, houses, papers, and effects, against unreasonable searches and seizures, shall not be violated, and no warrants shall issue, but upon probable cause, supported by oath or affirmation, and particularly describing the place to be searched, and the persons or things to be seized.

Since the initial interpretation of the Fourth Amendment by the Supreme Court in the late nineteenth century, the federal law of arrest, search, and seizure has developed into the most complicated of all the basic rights ensured in the Constitution. The reason for this is obvious. The amendment prohibits only unreasonable searches and seizures. A reasonable arrest, search, and seizure is a recognized, legitimate, and basic part of criminal-law enforcement. There are several hundred thousand arrests, searches, and seizures made each year. Yet any process so basic to the criminal law, particularly in a society that values the right to privacy, is bound to produce legal contests. Thus the federal courts have been called upon to decide what constitutes prior probable cause, who has the right of standing to raise the constitutional issue under the amendment, how extensive a reasonable search may be, what kinds of articles may be seized, and in what situation it is reasonable to dispense with securing a warrant. On the whole, the Supreme Court has been liberal in its protection of privacy under the amendment. In its first interpretation, the Court noted that while a particular unreasonable search or seizure might be divested of some of the more repulsive and aggravating incidents, such as the use of force, nonetheless:

> Illegitimate and unconstitutional practices get their first footing in that way, namely: by silent approaches and slight deviations from legal modes of procedure. This can only be obviated by adhering to the rule that constitutional provisions for the security of person and property should be liberally construed. . . . It is the duty of the courts to be watchful for the rights of the citizen and against any stealthy encroachments thereon.[17]

The *Weeks* rule of exclusion: the merging of the Fourth and Fifth Amendments The Supreme Court has been solicitous of the right of privacy not only because it values individual privacy but also because it has felt that most illegal searches and seizures are made for the purpose of compelling the individual to incriminate himself. In other words, forceful extortion of a person's private and lawful possessions is frequently for the purpose of using the papers and effects as evidence against him in a criminal case. In order to protect these Fourth and Fifth Amendment rights, the Court devised the *Weeks* rule, which excludes from trial evidence obtained in an unreasonable search and seizure.[18]

[16]Dissenting in *United States v. On Lee*, 193 F.2d 306, 351 (1951).
[17]*Boyd v. United States*, 116 U.S. 616, 635, (1886).
[18]*Weeks v. United States*, 232 U.S. 383 (1914).

The rule has been hotly contested since its inception. The opponents of the rule argue that it does not make sense to allow a criminal to go free simply because the police made an unreasonable search and seizure. They hold that the remedy adds nothing to the rights of the innocent person and is useful only to the law violator. Perhaps the most forceful critic of the Weeks-Mapp rule is Chief Justice Burger, who has written that:

> Some clear demonstration of the benefits and effectiveness of the exclusionary rule is required to justify it in view of the high price it extracts from society—the release of countless guilty criminals. . . . But there is no empirical evidence to support the claim that the rule actually deters illegal conduct of law enforcement officials. . . .
>
> There are several reasons for this failure. The rule does not apply any direct sanction to the individual official whose illegal conduct results in the exclusion of evidence in a criminal trial. With rare exceptions law enforcement agencies do not impose direct sanctions on the individual officer responsible for a particular judicial application of the supression doctrine. . . . Thus there is virtually nothing done to bring about a change in his practices. The immediate sanction triggered by the application of the rule is visited upon the prosecutor whose case against a criminal is either weakened or destroyed. The doctrine deprives the police in no real sense; except that apprehending wrongdoers is their business, police have no more stake in successful prosecutions than prosecutors or the public.
>
> . . . But the prosecutor who loses his case because of police misconduct is not an official in the police department; he can rarely set in motion any corrective action or administrative penalties. Moreover, he does not have control or direction over police procedures or police actions that lead to the exclusion of evidence.
>
> . . . Suppressing unchallenged truth has set guilty criminals free but demonstrably has neither deterred deliberate violations of the Fourth Amendment nor decreased those errors in judgment that will inevitably occur given the pressures inherent in police work having to do with serious crimes.[19]

The proponents of the *Weeks* rule argue that it is the only practical deterrent against unreasonable searches and seizures by the police. By denying the police any benefit from an illegal search and seizure, it is felt that the rule discourages illegal enforcement of the law. The *Weeks* rule has been in effect on the federal level for sixty years. There is little evidence to suport the contention that it is an effective deterrent in preventing unreasonable searches and seizures in the majority of cases. It has its most effective force in the area of serious criminal offenses where the police are interested in bringing a prosecution; in dealing with petty crimes its remedial value is doubtful. If the police have no serious intention of prosecuting an individual, they will not be constrained by a rule which can be felt only by denying them the use of illegal evidence in a prosecution. Additionally, the rule's effectiveness is dependent upon the police making an illegal seizure of articles, which can then be returned to the defendant or suppressed as evidence.

[19]Dissenting in *Bivens v. Six Unknown Named Agents*, 403 U.S. 388, 415–418 (1971).

The exclusionary rule does not provide a remedy for an illegal arrest per se, unaccompanied by any incidental search and seizure. The majority of arrests are not made with any intention of prosecution. The police look upon this illegal conduct in the area of petty crimes as a policy of harassment. They consider it a cheap and effective method of law enforcement. In short, the *Mapp* rule is not, as its critics often contend, a major roadblock to effective prosecution of crime. Indeed, a 1979 study by the General Accounting Office concluded that less than 1 percent of federal felony prosecutions were administratively screened out because of the exclusionary rule. Similarly, in less than 2 percent of federal cases filed for prosecution was evidence actually excluded under the rule. The results were approximately the same when the rule was examined at the state and local levels.[20]

Aside from its limited remedial value, the exclusionary rule has other justifications. From a moral viewpoint, many people feel that the government should follow a policy of "clean hands" in criminal-law enforcement; it should not stoop to the use of criminal tactics to enforce the law. Illegal enforcement of the law has a regressive element about it; it diminishes the respect for law in society.

THE SEESAW COURSE OF JUDICIAL INTERPRETATION

Although in the long run of legal history the judiciary has been generally sympathetic to the protection of privacy under the Fourth Amendment, the corollary exclusionary rule has had a troubled life. Even the Warren Court was at times skeptical about extending the rule. While it was the Warren Court that extended the rule to the states,[21] it was also the Warren Court that placed some limitations on its scope and efficacy. In 1963 a plurality of the Court indicated that the states would not be necessarily bound by the same rules relating to arrests and searches as applied in federal cases.[22] In 1967, with only Justice Douglas dissenting, the Court overturned a long-standing precedent that prohibited officers from seizing items that were of evidential value only.[23] And at the close of the Warren era the Court, again with only Justice Douglas dissenting, gave its approval to the common police practice of the warrantless "investigative stop and frisk." While the Court recognized this practice as "a serious intrusion upon the sanctity of the person," the majority agreed that the standard against which such intrusions would be judged was less than the heretofore-required "probable cause for arrest." Instead, the majority agreed that an officer's action would be judged by whether, at the moment of the seizure or search, a person of reasonable caution would conclude that such action was appropriate.[24] In effect, this loose post hoc standard gives the police relatively unrestrained freedom to proceed to "stop and frisk" individuals whose conduct may appear to be suspicious.

---

[20]See *Los Angeles Times*, July 1, 1979, pt. 1, p. 3.

[21]*Mapp v. Ohio*, 367 U.S. 643 (1961).

[22]*Ker v. California*, 374 U.S. 23, 31 (1963).

[23]*Gouled v. United States*, 255 U.S. 298 (1921), overturned in *Warden v. Hayden*, U.S. 294 (1957).

[24]*Terry v. Ohio*, 392 U.S. 1, 22 (1968).

The Burger Court, on the other hand, has been even less sensitive than the Warren Court to the issue of privacy. Since Justices Rehnquist and Powell joined the Court in early 1972, a new anti-Fourth Amendment majority has emerged. For example, in 1972, in a 6 to 3 decision, the Court extended the on-the-street "stop and frisk" rationale to situations where the officer had no firsthand knowledge, but rather acted on the tip of an unnamed informer, without any specification that the informer was reliable or had any firsthand knowledge of the situation.[25]

Two final cases will serve to illustrate further the serious erosion of privacy that is being sanctioned by the Court. In *United States v. Robinson*, an officer had reason to believe that a driver of a car did not have a valid operator's license. The officer stopped the car, arrested the driver, and conducted a full search of the driver, including a search of the contents of the driver's pockets. The search revealed a package of cigarettes, which, upon further investigation, contained capsules of heroin. In upholding the use of the heroin as evidence, the majority treated the search as merely a search incidental to an otherwise valid arrest.[26] The second case involves roughly parallel circumstances. An officer stopped an automobile because it moved across the center line three or four times. The driver was unable to produce his operator's license, and he was arrested for failure to have the license in his possession. Again a full body search was conducted, and again a package of cigarettes was found to contain narcotics, here marijuana. The traffic charge was dropped and the driver was convicted of unlawful possession.[27] Again, the majority treated the case as a simple search and seizure incident to an otherwise valid arrest.

It is easy to be misled by the aura of retroactive legitimacy of these cases. Yet the fact that the searches produced contraband should not divert attention from the fundamental issue of whether the searches were reasonable. In certain circumstances it is difficult to quarrel with the right, even necessity, of an officer to conduct a protective "frisk" for weapons at the moment of custodial arrest. But to suggest that arrest for minor traffic violations is cause for a full body search is farfetched. There are millions of cars on the streets and highways of America, and clearly there are thousands of violations of the vehicle codes. Large portions of these state codes attach misdemeanor or even felony status to violations that do not threaten life or property. Furthermore, the codes frequently confer on the police discretionary power to determine whether these violations will be handled by citation or arrest. It is also true that on any given day there will be several thousand drivers who will have on their persons evidence of a violation of a more serious offense. Subjecting a far greater number of drivers who may be in technical violation of a vehicle code to a search simply in order to catch those drivers who may be carrying evidence of serious offenses is a high price to pay for law enforcement, and yet the *Robinson* and *Gustafson* decision invite such a result.

Furthermore, assuming for purposes of argument that any search in minor vehicle code violations is valid, the scope of the searches sanctioned in these cases seems excessive. Search incidental to arrest has always been assumed to have its justification in protecting the safety of

[25]*Adams v. Williams*, 407 U.S. 143 (1972).
[26]*United States v. Robinson*, 94 S.Ct. 467 (1973).
[27]*Gustafson v. Florida*, 94 S.Ct. 488 (1973).

the officers, bystanders, and the arrestee. To sanction a search beyond an outer-clothing "pat down," at least where there is no initial suspicion or subsequent evidence of arms, is surely to make this an even more attractive option for officers in ferreting out crime and consequently to encourage its greater use. Since search incidental to a valid arrest has always been considered an exception to the requirement of a search warrant,[28] it seems appropriate that the judiciary should restrict the physical scope of these incidental searches in order not to encourage general or exploratory searches aimed at uncovering evidence of any crime. To do otherwise is to substantially diminish the expectation of privacy that millions of American automobile drivers are entitled to under the Fourth Amendment.

Couple the expanded scope of incidental physical search sanctioned in the above cases with the *Adams* rationale and one wonders if the Fourth Amendment has much vitality, outside of the home, for large numbers of Americans. This may sound unduly alarming, but consider for a moment the following: The *Adams* case greatly diminished the necessity for the police to give any justification for a "stop and frisk" by expanding the permissible situations to include "suspicious persons" unrelated to any observed conduct. Add to this the almost casual remark of Justice Rehnquist that the officer in the *Adams* case was patrolling in a "high crime" area, and further add that the Court has recently ruled that the voluntariness of a search is not dependent on whether one was aware of the legal right to refuse to consent to the search,[29] and then the Fourth Amendment takes on a certain existential meaning. Read "high crime" areas as poor neighborhoods, read lack of knowledge of constitutional rights as under-educated persons, particularly minorities and youth, read custodial arrest and search in minor traffic offenses as a blank check, and then it seems possible that the Court has sanctioned a kind of hunting license, unfamiliar to most middle-class Americans, but known and resented in the ghetto and barrio.

The *Terry* and *Adams* cases appeared to sanction an almost boundless authority for the police to act on mere suspicion and hunches. Yet neither of these cases directly addressed the issue of the standard to be applied in a forcible street-encounter stop. That question was finally addressed in a 1979 case, *Brown v. Texas*.[30] The facts of the case are simple. During an afternoon patrol, officers noticed Brown and another man walking in opposite directions away from one another in an alley. The patrol car entered the alley and the officers requested that Brown identify himself and explain his presence. The other man was not questioned or detained. The only justification offered by the officers was that the area was one of high drug traffic and Brown looked suspicious. Brown refused to identify himself. One of the officers then "frisked" him and found nothing, but the officers arrested Brown under a Texas statute that makes it a criminal offense to refuse to give one's name and address (when lawfully stopped) to the requesting peace officer. In overturning Brown's conviction the Court noted:

---

[28]See H. F. Way, "Increasing Scope of Search Incidental to Arrest," *Washington University Law Quarterly*, vol. 1959, no. 3, pp. 261–280.
[29]*Schneckloth v. Bustamonte*, 93 S.Ct. 2041 (1973).
[30]99 S.Ct. 2637.

We have recognized that in some circumstances an officer may detain a suspect briefly for questioning although he does not have "probable cause" to believe that the suspect is involved in criminal activity, as is required for a traditional arrest. However, we have required the officers to have a reasonable suspicion, based on objective facts, that the individual is involved in criminal activity. The flaw in the State's case is that none of the circumstances preceding the officers' detention of appellant justified a reasonable suspicion that he was involved in criminal conduct. . . . In the absence of any basis for suspecting appellant of misconduct, the balance between the public interest and appellant's right to personal security and privacy tilts in favor of freedom from police interference.[31]

The *Brown* decision, then, tethers *Terry*; officers may make investigatory stops but only when they are acting on a reasonable suspicion based on specific and objective facts.[32] Although investigatory stops interfere with individual liberty, they are not prohibited by the Fourth Amendment, nor should they be, but they must be done in reference to a constitutional standard and not on mere whim.

When we look back over the past sixty years of American legal history, it is difficult to escape the conclusion that but for the *Weeks-Mapp* rule, the Fourth Amendment could have become a museum piece. The general failure of the legislature and the executive to oversee the police and the failure to provide either meaningful civil remedies for illegal searches or strong administrative sanctions to discourage such searches constitutes a continuing justification for a rule that may well undermine police efficiency. Yet, to paraphrase Justice Brandeis, the Constitution was not adopted to promote efficiency but to preclude the exercise of arbitrary power.[33] This is an idea worth preserving.

THE *MIRANDA* RULE

The sacrifice of efficiency and ease to procedural restraint is not only evident in the *Weeks-Mapp* rule but also in the equally controversial *Miranda* rule announced in 1966.[34] The *Miranda* rule is the lineal descendant of a long effort in Anglo-American history aimed at the twin problems of arbitrary detention and coerced confessions. In 1628 Charles I gave his consent, begrudgingly, to the Petition of Right. One part of the petition urged that no freeman be detained by the king's command "without being charged with anything to which they might make answer according to law." Abritrary police detention becomes the foundation for the related problem of illegal confessions. It was also during the reign of Charles I that antecedents of the modern law against compulsory self-incrimination began to take shape. The indomitable "Free-born" John Lilburne, a Puritan zealot, when summoned in 1637 to testify before the Court of Star Chamber, refused to take the hated criminatory oath, for which he was fined and whipped and became something of a hero. At about the same time a maxim of uncertain origins, *nemo tenetur prodere seipsum*—"no one is

---

[31]Ibid., p. 2641; see United States *v.* Mendenhall, 100 S.Ct. 1870 (1980).
[32]See also *Delaware v. Prouse* for random automobile stops, 99 S.Ct. 1396 (1979).
[33]Dissenting in *Myers v. United States*, 272 U.S. 160, 293 (1926).
[34]*Miranda v. Arizona*, 384 U.S. 436 (1966).

bound to betray or accuse himself"—began to be heard in the common law courts. The criminatory oath and the maxim, though in origin unrelated, form the genesis of what gradually became the modern law against compulsory self-incrimination as embodied in the Fifth Amendment.[35]

For a number of years the Supreme Court attempted, with little success, to check the power of the police to arbitrarily detain suspects and interrogate them.[36] In state prosecutions, confessions obtained by physical coercion and confessions that were held to be the product of psychological coercion were held to be inadmissible as evidence.[37] At the federal level, the Court went even further, ruling in 1943 that confessions obtained by federal authorities without first promptly taking the accused before a committing magistrate were inadmissible.[38] Prompt arraignment of the accused was intended, the Court observed, not only to protect the innocent but to ensure that conviction of the guilty be done by methods "that commend themselves to a progressive and self-confident society. For this procedural requirement checks resort to those reprehensible practices known as the 'third degree' which, though universally rejected as indefensible, still find their way into use."[39]

Once the Warren Court incorporated the right of counsel and the right of no compulsory self-incrimination into the due process clause of the Fourteenth Amendment,[40] the next step was to combine these requirements into a rule that would exclude as evidence incriminating statements and admissions obtained without a warning of a suspect's right to counsel and to silence. This step was first taken in *Escobedo v. Illinois*[41] in 1964 and developed further in 1966 in *Miranda v. Arizona*. Briefly stated the Miranda rule provides that:

> The prosecution may not use statements, whether exculpatory or inculpatory, stemming from custodial interrogation of the defendant unless it demonstrates the use of procedural safeguards effective to secure the privilege against self-incrimination. By custodial interrogation, we mean questioning initiated by law enforcement officers after a person has been taken into custody or otherwise deprived of his freedom of action in any significant way. As for the procedural safeguards to be employed, unless other fully effective means are devised to inform accused persons of their right of silence and to assure a continuous opportunity to exercise it, the following measures are required. Prior to any questioning, the person must be warned that he has a right to remain silent, that any statement he does make may be used as evidence against him, and that he has a right to the presence of an attorney, either retained or appointed.

[35]See Lewis Mayers, *Shall We Amend the Fifth Amendment*, New York, Harper and Borthers, 1959, chap. 2.

[36]See H. F. Way, "The Supreme Court and State Coerced Confessions," *Journal of Public Law*, vol. 12, no. 1, 1963.

[37]*Brown v. Mississippi*, 297 U.S. 278 (1936), and *Chambers v. Florida*, 309 U.S. 227 (1940).

[38]*McNabb v. United States*, 318 U.S. 332 (1943), and *Mallory v. United States*, 354 U.S. 449 (1957).

[39]*McNabb v. United States*, 318 U.S. 343–344 (1943); the *McNabb-Mallory* rule was not based on any constitutional mandate, but rather on the power of the Courts to determine the rules of procedure in federal courts.

[40]*Gideon v. Wainwright*, 372 U.S. 335 (1963), and *Malloy v. Hogan*, 378 U.S. 1 (1964).

[41]*Escobedo v. Illinois*, 378 U.S. 478 (1964).

The defendant may waive effectuation of these rights, provided the waiver is made voluntarily, knowingly and intelligently. If, however, he indicates in any manner and at any stage of the process that he wishes to consult with an attorney before speaking there can be no questioning. Likewise, if the individual is alone and indicates in any manner that he does not wish to be interrogated, the police may not question him. The mere fact that he may have answered some questions or volunteered some statements on his own does not deprive him of the right to refrain from answering any further inquiries until he has consulted with an attorney and thereafter consents to be questioned.[42]

Impact of Miranda   As in the case of the *Weeks-Mapp* rule, opposition to the *Miranda* rule has been widespread. The opposition has focused on the wisdom of restraining the police and prosecutors in discharging their duty to question suspects and the likelihood that the rule will seriously impede the effectiveness of the police by foreclosing interrogation of suspects. However, the impact of *Miranda* appears to be minimal. Apparently in most jurisdictions some form of *Miranda* warning is being used, although not necessarily in full or at the required time. There is some evidence to suggest that when the warnings are given, they are neither disruptive of the process of interrogation nor likely to reduce the rate of felony convictions. There are a number of reasons for this. The *Miranda* decision did not, of course, prohibit police interrogation but only the trial use of confessions obtained in the absence of proper warnings during a custodial interrogation. Many suspects will want to talk to the police and will sometimes be advised by counsel to do so, particularly when there is some bargaining in regard to charges and recommended sentence. It should be noted also that confessions are not essential in the vast bulk of criminal cases.[43] Furthermore, suspects may not fully understand the warnings or may even conclude that because they were given the warnings by the police, the police are not their adversaries. Finally, Miranda requirements do not establish an insurmountable barrier to the use of confessions obtained in seeming violation of one or more requirements. Even if the police ignore the accused's request to remain silent, an incriminatory statement obtained may be admitted if the government can demonstrate at the trial that the statement was obtained after the accused knowingly and intelligently waived the right to silence.[44]

The fact that *Miranda* may have had limited impact on the behavior of police is not to suggest that the decision was unimportant or trivial. It is questionable whether a single court decision can alter conduct that is both pervasive and presumed by many to be reasonable. The importance of the decision rests not so much on its demonstrated efficacy as on its contribution to the ever-developing principle of legality. Interrogations, however important and necessary they may be, are, nonetheless, set in an atmosphere that is both coercive and calculated to trade on individual weaknesses—indeed, at times, to subjugate the suspect to the will of the examiner. Police interrogations, thus, run a high risk of producing results that are not the free choice of the suspect. The purpose of the rule is not a

---

[42]*Miranda v. Arizona*, 384 U.S. 444-445 (1966).
[43]For an analysis of the studies of the impact of *Miranda*, see Wasby, *The Impact of the United States Supreme Court*, pp. 154-162.
[44]384 U.S., p. 475.

misplaced sense of compassion for criminals, but rather a recognition that interrogations "exact a heavy toll on individual liberty,[45] and thus a prudential constitutional order will provide an advance check simply in order to reduce the likelihood of abuse. The rule is not intended to preclude interrogations and confessions, nor does it appear to have done so, but to warn the examiner that the power to arrest, interrogate, and charge is a public trust and not a matter of public faith.

The Burger Court and *Miranda* It was widely speculated after 1968 that a "Nixon Court" might overturn the *Miranda* decision. In a Dallas speech in May of 1968 Richard Nixon indicated that in his estimation the judiciary was partly responsible for the increase in crime, and he singled out for particular criticism the *Miranda* decision. Later in the campaign he said he would appoint justices who had great knowledge of the criminal law and an understanding of the role of some Supreme Court decisions in "weakening the peace forces" in our society.

Nixon did not appoint a majority to the Supreme Court. However, he did make four appointments, and these, combined with Justices Stewart and White, dissenters in the *Miranda* case, could overturn the decision. In 1971 the first of the Nixon appointees, Chief Justice Burger and Justice Blackman, joined three *Miranda* dissenters in a decision that tended to undercut the deterrent value of the rule. In *Harris v. New York* the new majority ruled that even though an incriminatory statement was inadmissible evidence under *Miranda*, nonetheless it could properly be used to attack the credibility of a defendant's trial testimony. In other words, while the prosecution may not directly introduce the statement, it may do so indirectly in order to demonstrate that the defendant's trial testimony is in conflict with the pretrial statement. However important it is to discourage perjury, the clear implication of the *Harris* decision is that the police may, with impunity, disregard the requirements of *Miranda*, knowing full well that the vast majority of defendants do find it desirable to testify at their own trials, and that the otherwise inadmissible statement or confession then can be introduced to impeach the credibility of the defendant's testimony. *Harris* may be useful in obtaining the conviction of felons, but it may also encourage arbitrary police behavior.[46]

While it does not seem likely that the present majority will directly overturn *Miranda*, it is probable that the Court will limit the impact, either directly, as attempted in the *Harris* case, or indirectly by neglecting to clarify certain areas. The *Miranda* rule, as originally announced, attempted to give greater advance precision than is customary in such situations. Still, the original rule leaves many questions unanswered, and in consequence there is more latitude under the rule than one might otherwise think. The Warren Court made only one major clarification of *Miranda*. In *Orozco v. Texas* the Court held that *Miranda* warnings were required not only in station-house interrogations but also in field interrogation.[47]

Two issues that need clarification are the meaning of *custodial* interrogation and whether partial or modified warnings are acceptable. *Miranda*

[45]*Miranda v. Arizona*, 384 U.S. 455 (1966).
[46]*Harris v. New York*, 401 U.S. 222 (1971); see also *Oregon v. Hass*, 420 U.S. 714 (1975).
[47]*Orozco v. Texas*, 394 U.S. 324 (1969); see also *Mathis v. United States*, 391 U.S. 1 (1968).

indicated that the required warnings are triggered by the fact one is either taken into custody or otherwise significantly deprived of freedom of action. Presumably, arrest will always trigger the warnings, but there are many situations short of arrest or prior to arrest that would also appear to qualify under the phrase "deprived of freedom of action in a significant way."[48] The failure of the Court to take jurisdiction in some of the numerous petitions filed annually would appear to indicate that it intends to allow the current latitude in custodial interrogation to continue.[49] Similarly the failure of the Court to take jurisdiction in cases involving partial or modified warnings, particularly in relation to the right of counsel, would seem to be an indication that the Burger Court is applying the brakes of judicial restraint to the *Miranda* rule.[50]

Restraint by neglect is not the only response that the Burger Court has made to *Miranda*. Indeed, the Court handed down two decisions in the 1970s that undermined the original rational of *Miranda*. In *Michigan v. Mosley*, a 1975 case, the defendant was arrested on a robbery charge and given *Miranda* warnings by Detective Cowie, whereupon he exercised his right to silence and was then placed in a cell. A few hours later another detective sought to question Mosley on a different charge. Mosley was again given *Miranda* warnings. This time he did not reassert his rights and made incriminating admissions that were introduced against him at his trial. The Supreme Court upheld the admission of the statements on the basis that any right to silence once exercised does not create a proscription of indefinite duration against any further interrogation.[51] The majority reasoned that since the police had honored Mosley's initial request to remain silent, and since the second interrogation was preceded by a second set of warnings and after a lapse of at least two hours from the original setting, the subsequent questioning did not undercut Mosley's initial request to remain silent. Of course the *Mosley* opinion is correct in asserting that the exercise of the right to silence ought not to create a blanket immunity from all subsequent interrogation. The opinion fails, however, to address the issue of continuing custody. Custody is the triggering device for *Miranda* warnings, and so long as custody continues or the accused remains uncounseled, the coercive atmosphere remains. It was this atmosphere that gave rise to *Miranda*, and nothing in the *Mosley* facts suggest that the *Miranda* predicate had been dispelled.

The second opinion, *North Carolina v. Butler*, a 1979 case, addressed the issue of whether a waiver of one's *Miranda* rights must be explicit.[52] Butler had been arrested by the FBI and read his *Miranda* warnings. When asked if he understood his rights he indicated he did, but he refused to sign the waiver form. He said he would talk to the agents but would not sign any form. He then made inculpatory statements. Subsequently he claimed that at the time the statements were made he had not waived his rights to an attorney. In upholding the admission the majority ruled that waivers may be explicit or implicit, and "The question is not one of form,

[48]See, for example, *Illinois v. Drumheller*, 304 N.E.2d 455 (1973); cf. *Arizona v. Mayes*, 518 P2d 568 (1974).
[49]For example, *Sicilia v. United States*, 475 F2d 308 (1973), cert. denied 10/9/73.
[50]For example, *Sundry v. United States*, 474 F2d 1397 (1973), cert. denied 10/9/73.
[51]423 U.S. 96 (1975).
[52]99 S.Ct. 1755.

but rather whether the defendant in fact knowingly and voluntarily waived the rights delineated in the *Miranda* case. As was unequivocally said in *Miranda*, mere silence is not enough. That does not mean that the defendant's silence, coupled with an understanding of his rights and a course of conduct indicating waiver, may never support a conclusion that a defendant has waived his rights.[53]

Once again the Court's majority has ignored an important feature of *Miranda*. The *Miranda* rules were intended to dispel the evidentiary disputes that generally surrounded confession cases in the 1940s and 1950s. Given the incommunicado setting of police interrogations, disputes as to what actually occurred are inevitable. The *Butler* decision, by allowing trial courts to determine waiver by inferences drawn from ambiguous words or gestures, once again returns to the typical pre-*Miranda* problem of factual disputes.

THE CONSTITUTIONAL RIGHTS OF PRISONERS

Until just over a decade ago the legal rights of prisoners was a topic of only minor concern to the legal profession and of almost no concern to the judiciary. It was, in fact, a wasteland in constitutional law. That prisons were sometimes exposed as dark and evil aroused little concern.[54] After all, for much of our history we had treated prisoners as little more than chattels, souls dead to the law. Indeed, even the Thirteenth Amendment, prohibiting slavery and involuntary servitude, exempts its proscription when applied to the punishment of crime. Of course, a sentence to a prison necessarily entails the surrender of many liberties that one valued in the outside world. Correctional authorities must have a degree of control over the daily lives of prisoners that may not be exercised over nonprisoners. While it may be true that we send many persons to prison who should receive other forms of treatment, the fact is that prisons are sometimes the only solution society has for those who threaten life, safety, and property. Yet an individual's inability to cope with freedom has not, at least in the history of Anglo-American law, been thought to justify turning prisons into barbarous nightmares.

Some consequences of convictions The loss of immediate personal liberty that attends incarceration is not necessarily the only consequence of a prison sentence. Some jurisdictions impose harsh civil disabilities and disqualifications on convicted felons.[55] The collateral consequences of a felony conviction may be temporary or permanent and may encompass such matters as the right to hold public office, to vote, to serve on a jury, to give sworn testimony, to transfer or inherit property, and to practice certain professions.

While some collateral consequences may appropriately apply during the period of incarceration, it is difficult to justify the sometimes perma-

---

[53]Ibid., p. 1757.
[54]See, for example, the background facts in *Hutto v. Finney*, 437 U.S. 678 (1978).
[55]For a listing of disabilities, see "The Collateral Consequences of Criminal Convictions," *Vanderbilt Law Review*, vol. 23, p. 929, 1970.

nent loss of certain rights. Thus, the permanent disenfranchisement of ex-felons appears to offer little social utility. Society might well conclude that it would be desirable to deny the vote to those ex-felons convicted of election fraud, but what social purpose is served by denying the vote to those convicted of violating narcotics laws? Although a majority of the states do not permanently disenfranchise ex-felons, yet as recently as 1974 the Supreme Court held that such a disability does not violate the equal protection clause. In *Richardson v. Ramirez* the Court, Justice Rehnquist writing for the majority, ruled that a little-known provision of the Fourteenth Amendment gave affirmative sanction to the permanent disenfranchisement of ex-felons.[56] Section II of the amendment says that the number of representatives to Congress that a state is entitled to may be reduced if the state denies or abridges the right of male citizens twenty-one years old to vote *except* where the abridgment is "for participation in rebellion or other crime." While the historical record is clear as to what Congress intended when it wrote the proviso about participating in rebellion, the record fails to clarify what "other crime" was intended to cover. At this point in time the proviso appears to be little more than a historical accident, not unlike the Thirteenth Amendment proviso that slavery is prohibited except as punishment for crime. Surely the Court would not seize upon this Thirteenth Amendment clause as a justification for allowing a state to turn prisoners into slaves. The historical context and textual exegesis are by no means the only accepted methods of interpreting constitutional provisions. The Court has some responsibility to insure that constitutional provisions, such as the due process and equal protection clauses, are allowed to evolve. Justice Rehnquist's caveat in the *Richardson* case that it is not the responsibility of the Court to choose one set of values over the other will satisfy *only* those who still believe in mechanical jurisprudence.[57]

Fundamental legal rights of prisoners   We cannot attempt here a compendium of the constitutional rights of prisoners, but we can indicate that prisons do not operate outside the Constitution and that prisoners do not lose all of their constitutional rights. One of the most fundamental rights retained is access to the courts.[58] Clearly, access to the courts is often essential if prisoners are to be allowed to pursue any remaining legal rights regarding their convictions and sentences, or to petition concerning the conditions of confinement or their status as prisoners. The Court has even ruled that prisoners are entitled to a reasonably adequate law library[59] and adequate legal assistance in the preparation and filing of meaningful legal papers.[60]

Whether prisoners have an absolute and unrestricted right to file any civil action they desire is, however, questionable. Until recently many states had so-called civil death statutes under which the civil and political rights of incarcerated felons were suspended. The suspension generally

[56]418 U.S. 24.
[57]See 418 U.S. at 55.
[58]See *Ex parte Hull*, 312 U.S. 546 (1941).
[59]*Younger v. Gilmore*, 404 U.S. 15 (1971).
[60]See *Wolff v. McDonnell*, 418 U.S. 539 (1974), and *Bounds v. Smith*, 430 U.S. 817, 827–829 (1977).

included denial of access to the courts on any matter not related to the prisoner's conviction or sentence. The rationale for this was that unless prisoner access to the courts was limited, "penitentiary wardens and the the courts might be swamped with an endless number of unnecessary and even spurious law suits filed by inmates in remote jurisdictions in the hope of obtaining leave to appear at the hearing . . . with the consequent disruption of prison routine and concomitant hazard of escape from custody."[61] A 1977 Supreme Court decision would appear to cast doubt on any absolute bar to prisoner access to the courts on the normal civil matters confronted by many prisoners, such as divorce, child custody, and debtor problems.[62] While there may be compelling state interests that require some constraints on prisoner access to the courts, nonetheless, the old civil death statutes raise serious problems under both due process and equal protection, especially where they operate to deprive prisoners or parolees of property rights.[63]

Meaningful access to the courts often requires legal expertise not possessed by prisoners. For some time the Supreme Court has held that on the right of first appeal to attack a conviction, an indigent is entitled to free legal counsel and free transcripts,[64] but a 1974 decision would appear to exclude such assistance beyond the first appellate court review.[65] Furthermore, while the Court has held that revocation of probation or parole must conform to due process fairness requirements, this does not mean that fairness will necessarily require the presence of prisoner counsel.

A more debatable problem concerns the degree of procedural regularity and fairness that is required in prison disciplinary proceedings. Given the wide range and character of prison discipline and the importance of discipline to prison security, there is an evident need for substantial administrative discretion. In *Wolff v. McDonnell* (1974), the Court ruled that certain minimum due process requirements apply to disciplinary procedures that are aimed at taking away an important state-created prisoner right, such as good-time credit.[66] Subsequent Supreme Court decisions have questioned the application of due process standards to disciplinary *proceedings*.[67] On the other hand certain disciplinary *practices*, such as physical punishment, would come within the ban on cruel and unusual punishment. Indeed, in 1970 a federal district court ruled that an entire penitentiary system was in violation of the ban on cruel and unusual punishment.[68]

The First Amendment and prisoners   Traditionally prisoners have had to surrender substantial rights under the First Amendment. The normal

---

[61]*Tabor v. Hardwick*, 224 F.2d 526, 529 (1955).
[62]*Bounds v. Smith*, 430 U.S. 817, 827 (1977).
[63]See *Bush v. Reid*, 516 P.2d 1215, Alas S.Ct. (1973).
[64]*Douglas v. California*, 372 U.S. 353 (1963), and *Griffin v. Illinois* 351 U.S. 12 (1956).
[65]*Ross v. Moffitt*, 417 U.S. 600.
[66]Ibid., 418 U.S. 539.
[67]For example, *Baxter v. Palmigiamo*, 425 U.S. 308 (1979).
[68]See *Holt v. Sarver*, 309 F. Supp. 362 (E. D. Ark), aff'd sub nom. *Hutto v. Finney*, 437 U.S. 678 (1978); cf. *United States v. Bailey*, 100 S.Ct. 624 (1980), where a majority ruled that before deplorable conditions of jail confinement will be accepted as justification for escape, the escaped prisoner must show a bona fide effort to return to custody as soon as claimed conditions lose their coercive force.

avenues for the exercise of freedom of speech, press and association would often be inconsistent with the status of being a prisoner. While prison authorities may conclude the penological objectives are well served by allowing an inmate-operated prison newspaper, normal constitutional rights of advocacy of ideas—as, for example, the utility of prison riots in improving prison conditions—would hardly apply to such an inmate newspaper. As the Supreme court noted some years ago, "lawful incarceration brings about the necessary withdrawal or limitation of many privileges and rights, a retraction justified by the considerations underlying our penal system."[69]

The foregoing statement of the Court remains an entirely reasonable one. But when the statement is coupled with the judiciary's natural reluctance to intrude into administrative areas, it has often meant that courts were unwilling to address the denial of certain constitutional rights of prisoners, rights not inconsistent with the status of prisoners. True, one cannot lift First Amendment law out of its natural environment and place it within the confines of a maximum-security prison. Yet there are a few First Amendments rights that may be exercised within prisons that need not undermine either prison discipline or penological objectives. Thus freedom of religious exercise has been a customary part of prison life. It is an open question whether the state must provide prison religious facilities and chaplains, although states have traditionally done so for mainline Christian-sects and the Jewish faith, and at state expense. If, however, the state extends a measure of religious freedom for conventional religious groups to operate in a prison, then it must extend a similar freedom to nonconventional sects.[70] Of course, this assumes that the form of religious exercise is not inconsistent with prison discipline and penological objectives. Freedom of worship within a prison is not an invitation to prison con-artists to demand steak and red wine for a sacramental ceremony.

Beyond the right of religious worship, the Court has also indicated that prisoners retain certain rights as senders and recipients of mail. In striking down California prison regulations governing prisoner mail, the Court ruled:

> that censorship of prisoner mail is justified if the following criteria are met. First, the regulation or practice in question must further an important or substantial government interest unrelated to the suppression of expression. Prison officials may not censor inmate correspondence simply to eliminate unflattering or unwelcome opinions or factually inaccurate statements. Rather, they must show that a regulation authorizing mail censorship furthers one or more of the substantial government interests of security, order, and rehabilitation. Second, the limitation of First Amendment freedoms must be no greater than is necessary or essential to the protection of the particular governmental interest involved.[71]

Some weeks after the unanimous decision in *Procunier v. Martinez* the Court handed down additional prison-regulation decisions that refused

[69]*Price v. Johnson*, 334 U.S. 266, 285 (1948).
[70]*Cruz v. Beto*, 405 U.S. 319 (1972).
[71]*Procunier v. Martinez*, 416 U.S. 396, 413 (1974).

to extend a First Amendment right to prisoners to initiate interviews with representatives of the press.[72] A now-divided Court held that the medium of written correspondence available to prisoners affords them an open and substantially unrestricted method for communication with persons outside prison and, therefore, content-neutral restrictions on prisoner access to press were not unconstitutional. However, in a 1977 decision the Court also upheld a North Carolina regulation prohibiting prisoners from receiving bulk-mail packets intended for redistribution to other inmates.[73] The 1977 decision involved a prisoners' labor union which was attempting, through collective bargaining, to improve prison working conditions and to act as the conduit for the presentation of prisoner grievances. The correctional agency had concluded that such a union would be detrimental to prison security and order and had refused to recognize it or to accord the union any prison privileges, including the privilege of holding organizational meetings.

Correctional agencies may *well* be right in their conclusion that a prisoner union would be detrimental to prison security and order or that prisoners should not be allowed to initiate interviews with the press. Yet prison riots, such as the ones in Attica and New Mexico, suggest that there are prison conditions that require public exposure. How can pressure be placed on public authorities to examine prison conditions? The prisoners' solution often is to demand First Amendment rights and then to air publicly their grievances. The difficulty with this solution is that once a constitutional right has been accorded prisoners, we would expect it to operate in much the same manner as in the free world. In the free world the exercise of a constitutional right is not conditioned on the substantive use to which it will be put. Thus, if prisoners were accorded a constitutional right to organize, could that right be withdrawn when a union's substantive demands were thought to be inconsistent with prison order? If the demands were rejected, it would be utopian to assume that a prisoner union would then passively accept the rejection.

It may be sound penology for correctional agencies to allow some form of inmate association, even a union, but it would be an arguable constitutional proposition. On the other hand, it would seem equally unsound to isolate constitutional access to prisons and prisoners. The long-standing judicial policy of "hands off" prisons and prisoners proceeded from the mistaken assumption that the judiciary had no proper role to play in this area. A minimum constitutional solution to the Attica syndrome is to insure public awareness of prison conditions, and that goal cannot be accomplished if the Court continues to lock the press out of prisons. Due regard for prison security and order does not require that everything justified in the name of prison order and security be accepted by the courts.

CONCLUSION

In this chapter we have examined portions of two distinct areas of the criminal process—the pretrial and posttrial stages. Both of these stages are administered by executive officials, and each stage is marked by

[72]*Pell v. Procunier*, 417 U.S. 817 (1974); see also *Saxbe v. Washington Post*, 417 U.S. 843 (1974).
[73]*Jones v. North Carolina Prisoners' Labor Union*, 433 U.S. 119 (1977).

widespread acceptance and use of discretionary power. Discretionary power is often the antithesis of the procedural regularity that governs the trial stage of the criminal process. Police, prosecutors, and correctional officers justify their wide discretion as essential to their roles. The apprehension of suspected criminals, the screening and processing of suspects prior to trial or plea bargaining, and the subsequent care and custody of felons often taken place under conditions that cannot be predicted and consequently defy excessive procedural regularity. Clearly the procedural regularity and standards of fairness that govern much of the trial stage would be inappropriate at other stages of the criminal process. Yet this common-sense proposition cannot be used to justify every exercise of discretionary power by police, prosecutors, and correctional officers. We live under a constitutional system, and this necessarily means that all components must operate under constitutional restraints.

The constitutional proscriptions against unreasonable searches and seizures and against compulsory self-incrimination were not adopted as mere window-dressing for an otherwise arbitrary and authoritarian regime. Nor did we adopt a constitutional system in which felons could be consigned to legal oblivion. Yet the difficulty with these constitutional proscriptions is that they must compete with other societal goals that stress order and safety, and the latter goals are generally the ones that have organized political clout. In our legal culture, the effort to preserve and vitalize the restraints on the exercise of power by wardens, police, and prosecutors is not a sought-after assignment. Popularly elected officials often avoid any appearance of restraining law enforcement and corrections.

Sometimes, then, the only institution in our system that is capable of reviewing the claims for extensive unchecked executive power is the judiciary. Judicial checks on police and prosecutor power often take the form of exclusionary rules. Such rules exact a high price, one that society is rarely prepared to pay, and in consequence the judiciary is often reluctant to impose them. Not only do such rules help to free felons, but they place a certain unfair onus on the judiciary. It appears that the Burger Court would like to put a safe distance between the Court and these unpopular restraints on police and prosecutors. The solution to the issue is not, however, to repeal the rules, unless they are counterproductive to the deterrent goal. Instead, the solution is to make the rules unnecessary. This could be done, at a price, if the nonjudicial branches of government would assume responsibility for monitoring the police and prosecutors. The wide discretionary power exercised by police and prosecutors, coupled with the present lack of effective oversight and accountability, provide continuing justification for the kinds of judicially imposed restraints represented by exclusionary rules; modify these conditions and the need for such negative rules will disappear.

In all candor, the elected branches of government are not likely to develop a new sense of public responsibility for checking police-prosecutor power. On the other hand, the judiciary need not assume that public officials cannot be moved to respond to prison problems. At least if the judiciary keeps the the doors of prisons sufficiently open to the press, there is some reason to hope that public officials will react in a responsible manner.

6 EPILOGUE

Throughout the pages of this book it has been stressed that the judiciary, and especially the United States Supreme Court, has an important constitutional role in promoting and safeguarding civil liberties. Yet the judiciary, with neither the power of the purse nor the power of the sword, does not have a formidable array of weapons with which to discharge its responsibilities. The adversary process constrains the judiciary, often consigning it to a reactive role in our national life. The nature of a court as an institution for resolving disputed facts and law does not comport with the normal requirements of major public policy-making institutions in our society. The judiciary, for example, has only a feeble information-gathering power. The immediate litigants to a dispute, particularly a constitutional-level dispute, rarely represent all of the points of view that pertain to a dispute, nor can the immediate litigants make any claim that they give a court all of the information necessary to a complete understanding of a constitutional issue. Indeed, the rules of evidence have evolved in a manner designed to restrain the amount of information that a court can accept. In short an argument can be made against the judiciary, including the Supreme Court, playing an active policy-making role in our system of government.

Yet the institutional constraints on the judiciary are only one side of the coin. While the judiciary may be the least powerful branch of government, nonetheless it is not without power. Federal judges as well as many state judges have life tenure, a device intended to remove the judiciary from the vicissitudes of public opinion and the restraints of the elective process. While life tenure does not confer divinity on a judge, it does remove a judge from immediate accountability to the political process. This freedom enables the judicial process to be a more principled process, a process less immediately concerned with voter sentiment. The judicial process is indeed political, but it is political at a distance far removed from electoral accountability. Tenure, then, affords the judiciary greater latitude in assuming risks.

Of course, the judiciary must cast an occasional glance at the barometers of public opinion, but public opinion cannot be the cutting edge in exercising judgment. When Justice Holmes suggested that the life of the law is not logic but experience, surely he did not mean that the law must be a mirror image of the current social and political scene.

First of all, no such single mirror exists. In a highly pluralistic society the judiciary would be unable to turn to a single representation of current culture. Secondly, a legal system that merely catered to vocal groups would lose its capacity to lead.

The appellate judiciary has a special responsibility to lead in the development and renewal of constitutional principles. If one looks back over the past thirty years of constitutional history, it is evident that in many areas the Supreme Court acted well in advance of the political and social culture. The early cases narrowing the law of obscenity came before, not after, the sexual revolution of the 1960s. *Brown v. Topeka Board of Education* (1954) not only helped to spur the civil rights movement but it anticipated the revolution in personal rights by at least a decade. Even in those situations where the Court's decisions may have fallen initially on less fertile ground, for example, the prayer and Bible-reading cases, the Court's leadership has been largely responsible for the changes in religious practices in public schools. Public schools today are far more sensitive to the problems of religious pluralism and the nonbeliever than prior to those decisions.

Of course, it is true that the idea of an aggressive, active, and independent judiciary may be challenged on democratic grounds. The independence of the judiciary necessarily means that it is not politically accountable in the electoral sense. An active judiciary runs the risk of being out of step with majority sentiment. But then American democratic theory has never held that the majority should have the last word in government. For example, the Bill of Rights is an anti-majoritarian document intended to restrain the electoral branches of government and thereby protect certain important interests of those who may find themselves in a minority.

Judicial enforcement of the Bill of Rights and the Fourteenth Amendment is often the only protection available to the dispossessed and politically powerless. This is not to suggest that the strength of a constitutional claim should be measured by the social and political characteristics of the claimant. All that is suggested here is that the nature and structure of our political system does not require that courts be obsessed with self-restraint. The fact that the judiciary can make mistakes in constitutional policy is not a sufficient argument to support judicial abandonment of the Bill of Rights. Perhaps there are areas—for example, the economic area—where the judiciary is less able to make an effective contribution. On the other hand, there are areas of constitutional policy in which the judiciary has demonstrated institutional capability. For example, the *Brown* decision and the prayer and Bible-reading decisions, provided judicial leadership on issues that were at least temporarily beyond executive and legislative resolution. Even in the publicly sensitive area of the constitutional rights of criminal defendants, the judiciary's leadership remains vital. Prior to the Warren Court, the scales of justice had been tipped far too heavily in favor of the prosecution; some institutional response was necessary, and political realities indicated that the legislative and executive branches would not be able to place criminal justice on their agendas.

To argue in favor of continued judicial activism in civil liberties does not mean that judicial leadership will always be wise, and certainly the judiciary is not beyond criticism. For example, the judiciary can become trapped in its own policy. The controversy over busing is a case in point. For almost fifty years the Supreme Court has played a prominent and ever decisive role in establishing the rights of blacks as an item on the national agenda. The judiciary was the first forum of government to give legitimacy to the claims of blacks. Since the *Brown* decision in 1954 the Supreme Court has often acted as the national spokesperson for blacks. There is an almost institutional bond that unites the Court and the black community. The bond may have trapped some members of the Court in the area of desegregation. Thus, if the Court were now to insist that busing orders be predicated in de jure acts of segregation and that the orders attempt to correct only the results of de jure segregation, this could be construed as signaling the end of judicial support for blacks. Certainly blacks continue to suffer the adverse social and economic consequences of slavery and Jim Crowism. Much remains to be done, and consequently a shift in the direction of the Court on busing could have undesirable side-effects. Yet it would be a dubious constitutional policy to order mandatory school busing plans that are not based on a casual connection between the established fact of racial imbalances in the schools and proven racially segregative acts of school authorities.

To return to the issue of judicial activism in civil liberties, it should be noted that demands for self-restraint are often thinly disguised arguments against the protection of civil liberties. If the judiciary reduces its docket in any area of the law by refusing to hear cases, it may be motivated by constituional theories of deference to the political branches and to federalism. Certainly since the late 1930s the Court has been deferential to Congress on most economic issues. The "switch in time that saved nine" still has currency. It is also true, especially in the area of civil liberties, that it is easier to defend the status quo by the rubric of judicial self-restraint than it is to hear a case on its merits. The sophistry of self-restraint in civil liberties is particularly obvious in those areas where the judiciary is not deferring to any ongoing attempt by the states or the political branches to resolve problems in personal rights. Thus, the "hands-off" prison policy long adhered to by the judiciary could not be justified by deference to ongoing efforts by correctional agencies to resolve some serious and rather fundamental denials of basic human rights in American prisons. What efforts that did exist were usually feeble and without wide legislative support.

The essence of the above argument is that the judiciary has a special responsibility to ensure that the constitutional rights of the powerless and dispossessed are protected. But the argument for judicial activism in civil liberties does not flow solely from a need to protect the powerless or the dispossessed. Even if we assume for the moment that all groups have equal access to political power, there will still be disputes in civil liberties that require constitutional adjudication. Over the past twenty-five years, Roman Catholics have achieved substantial political power, and they have successfully used that power in many states to demand a share of the public tax monies to support parochial eduacation. Their claims to distributive justice are not without merit, but direct public support of religious education raises a serious constitutional issue that is almost invariably neglected in the legislative debates over the passage of state aid bills. Since a number of state legislatures have continued to pass such legislation, one could argue that the Court should defer to the wisdom of the states in this matter. Yet the mere fact that states persist in passing legislation to aid parochial schools is not ipso facto evidence of wisdom. Unless we are prepared to accept the Jeffersonian thesis that each branch of government is capable of making a final resolution of constitutional issues, then we are still pressed with Chief Justice Marshall's practical argument in favor of judicial resolution of constitutional conflicts. Once we accept the theory of judicial review we necessarily accept the possibility of judicial activism. Unless and until we can find other agencies of the government at once willing and able to address and resolve constitutional disputes and to do so more effectively than the courts, some measure of judicial activism must remain in our system.

Indeed it is possible to argue that it is only through judicial activism that certain constitutional claims are given a forum for resolution. But for judicial activism in civil liberties the Oliver Browns and Steven Engels might never have had an opportunity to have their claims aired. While constitutional issues are occasionally addressed by legislative and executive bodies, generally such issues are far from the mainstream of their concerns. The nature of both executive decision-making and the legislative process often works to encourage the avoidance of constitutional concerns, albeit with the expectation that such thorny problems are best left to the courts. As a general proposition it is quite likely that popularly elected or controlled bodies find it institutionally difficult to be sensitive to issues in civil liberties. Thus, judicial self-restraint cannot be posited on any notion that popular branches of government, in the normal course of policy-making, give full consideration to the constitutional problems arising out of a proposed policy.

Within the past decade a number of complaints have arisen about judicial activism, even judicial arrogance, involving certain decisions in the social and environmental arenas. The cry of "government by judiciary" may be entirely appropriate when certain of these decisions are examined. What should be avoided, however, is allowing this debate to spill over into the role of the judiciary in safeguarding the Bill of Rights.

As Jefferson noted, the Bill of Rights, like all human blessings, has its inconveniences. Yet the Bill of Rights and certain other amendments strike a prudential chord in our system of government. The power and energy of government today might cause even a Stuart monarch or an Alexander Hamilton to pause. It is capable of accomplishing much that is good. But free people cannot gamble their liberties on the chance that the powerful machinery of the state will not become abusive and arbitrary. The system of constitutional rights acts as the wise restraint on the zeal of officials and public passions. But the documents of our liberties cannot alone preserve our freedoms. As Woodrow Wilson noted, "Liberty is not something than can be laid away in a document a completed work. It is an organic principle,—a principle of life, renewing and being renewed. . . . It is a strenuous thing, this living the life of a free people."[1]

[1]Woodrow Wilson, *An Old Master and Other Political Essays*, New York, Scribner's, 1893, pp. 115–116.

INDEX

INDEX

63201

HIEBERT LIBRARY

3 6877 00146 7496

DATE DUE

JC   63201
599
.U5   Way, H. Frank
W35   Liberty in the
1981   balance.

HIEBERT LIBRARY
Fresno Pacific College - M.B. Seminary
Fresno, CA 93702

DEMCO